THE
APS
RECRUITMENT
GAME

A Practical Guide to
Sharpen Your Strategy,
Learn the Rules, and
Progress Your Public Service Career

Brendon Le Lievre

Quietly Loud Publishing

The APS Recruitment Game.

Written by Brendon Le Lievre.

First Edition, 2026

First published in Australia in 2026 by Quietly Loud Publishing.

A catalogue record for this book is available from the National Library of Australia

For Theodore and Fletcher.

May your careers and lives be rich in meaning and light on regret. Always back yourselves, keep learning, and walk into every new opportunity with confidence.

For Simone.

Thanks for continually encouraging me to do things outside of my comfort zone and supporting me to make brave choices.

My sincere thanks to Michelle, whose generous knowledge sharing and in depth guidance significantly shaped the final version of this book.

Thanks also to Bronwyn, Casey, Dave, Debbie, Felicity, Jason and Mia who read drafts and provided feedback and meaningful suggestions to content, structure and layout.

WELCOME

The reality is that most people are not in the job they will retire from and therefore have at least one more recruitment process to go through. If you don't enjoy the Australian Public Service (APS) recruitment process, that can be challenging to think about. Perhaps you struggle to write your pitch, find it awkward to talk about yourself, get nervous in interviews or are unsure what panels are looking for, my goal is to help you feel less overwhelmed and better equipped. If you are highly capable and do excellent work, this book is designed to help you navigate the process with greater clarity and confidence.

Recruitment is not about who you are.
It is about how well you can show it.

In many ways, APS recruitment is a game. When you understand the rules, have a strategy, practise your skills and play by them, you significantly increase your chances of success.

Would you play a new board game without reading the rules or having them explained to you and expect to feel comfortable? Would you play in a Grand Final with no training, no preparation and no regular season games under your belt and expect to perform at your best? Of course not, yet when it comes to recruitment, these are strategies that many people use. Recruitment processes make people uncomfortable, so they avoid preparing, skip practise and hope they somehow get through it and land the job.

Most people are unsuccessful in recruitment because they haven't learned how to play the game.

This book helps you better understand the rules so you can demonstrate your value in a process built on structure, focussed on behavioural evidence, and consistent assessment, drawing on my experience as a chair, panel member, and scribe.

Even if you do everything well, you won't get every job you apply for, but when you move away from guesswork and apply the frameworks in this book, you'll feel calmer, more confident and better able to present your skills, knowledge and experience at each stage of the process.

There is also an ethical question about this book that I want to address. Some people suggest that developing recruitment skills means the person who plays the game best gets the job, rather than the person best suited to the role. In reality, that imbalance already exists and those who are naturally confident, articulate, or experienced in recruitment often perform better, regardless of their organisational, team or role fit. One of the reasons I wrote this book is to help level that playing field.

Let's learn how to play the game.

TABLE OF CONTENTS

INTRODUCTION

My career in the APS was successful and deeply fulfilling, largely because the work was always connected to something bigger than just my role. I could see how what I was doing contributed to outcomes that mattered, and that created a strong sense of purpose for me. I also valued the standards the APS holds itself to. The emphasis on integrity, accountability and service shaped how I approached my work and informed the expectations placed on me and my colleagues. I'm now lucky enough through my work as a leadership development consultant to see this across multiple organisations while supporting public servants to pursue their potential and have more impact in the work that they do.

The APS is a very appealing place to work and that means recruitment is competitive and requires a deliberate approach. It is not enough to be the best qualified or experienced person in the process, you need to be prepared and clearly communicate what you can bring to the role, team and organisation.

That might sound frustrating and like a lot of work, but here's some good news, preparation is something you can control. The quickest way to secure a new role is to focus on presenting a clear and compelling case for why you are the best candidate. If you want to spend less time going through recruitment processes, it's worth leaning in for a period, preparing well, approaching it with intent, and securing that next role.

> *The impediment to action*
> *advances action.*
> *What stands in the way*
> *becomes the way.*
> *- Marcus Aurelius*

Done well, this short-term focus can lead to a role that better fits your strengths and gives you space to step out of the recruitment cycle for a while.

Applying for roles in the Australian Public Service can feel like learning another language. There are selection criteria, pitches, STAR models, Integrated Leadership System (ILS) frameworks, interview panels, bulk rounds, merit pools and referee checks. Add in the pressure of wanting to progress in your career and it is no wonder many people feel overwhelmed and/or underprepared and performance suffers.

After sitting on hundreds of APS recruitment panels, I learned that most capable candidates miss out not because they lack talent, but because they misunderstand how the system works.

A fair system will still reward those who understand how it works more than those who do not.

Once you understand how recruitment decisions are made, your preparation becomes far more focused. Instead of guessing what panels want, you can begin to present your experience in ways that match the way they assess candidates.

Panels are assessing behaviour using the evidence provided to determine whether someone can perform the role at the required level and a good fit for the team and organisation.

To do this they follow structured guidance, policies, processed and frameworks that are publicly available for you to learn from.

This book outlines a practical approach to preparing for APS recruitment processes, from deciding what your next move should be, identifying whether a role is right for you through to reflecting after an interview to gain insights on what to do next time. You will learn how to translate your experience into clear evidence that panels can assess.

Inside this book you will find:

- guidance on how to determine what the next move in your career should be
- an approach to deciding whether a role is actually right for you
- practical explanations of how to use the Integrated Leadership System and the STAR framework
- reflection activities to help identify your skills, knowledge and experience
- prompts to help develop strong examples for selection criteria and interviews

- stories drawn from my own experience as an applicant, panel chair, panel member and scribe

- suggestions on questions you should ask at the end of your interview

- how to maximise the contribution of your referee.

Inside the interview room

Throughout the book you will see short stories from *Inside the Interview Room*. These are drawn from real recruitment processes that I have participated in, or others have shared with me. The organisations and people have been anonymised, but the situations themselves are real.

My hope is that you learn from these stories. Some highlight examples of candidates who prepared well and demonstrated their capability clearly. Others show how small mistakes or misunderstandings can negatively affect the outcome of a recruitment process.

Adopting a Growth Mindset

In everything, including recruitment, your mindset shapes how you approach every situation, choose the actions you take and interpret every outcome. Drawing on the work of Carol Dweck in Mindset, I'd like to encourage you to adopt a Growth Mindset rather than a Fixed Mindset.

A Fixed Mindset assumes your ability is static, you either have what it takes or you don't. This can show up as thinking "I'm not good at interviews" or "I never get through shortlisting," which often leads to avoidance or frustration about the process.

A Growth Mindset, on the other hand, sees capability as something that can be developed through effort, feedback, and practise. It shifts the focus from judgement to learning, asking "What can I improve next time?" or "What did this process teach me?"

One simple but powerful way to make that shift is to add the word "yet." Instead of "I'm not good at recruitment," try "I'm not good at recruitment yet." It creates space for development and reminds you that skill in this area is built, not fixed.

Even if you apply everything in this book perfectly, you will not win every job you apply for, no one does or can.

What you will do is more consistently present the best version of your experience and capability in every recruitment process you participate in. Over time, that preparation significantly increases your chances of recruitment success and winning your next role.

So, let's begin at the very first step, defining what the next move in your career might be.

CHAPTER 1:
What is your next move?

Many of us were taught to think about careers as ladders. You start at the bottom, work hard, prove yourself, and steadily climb upwards. Each step is bigger, better, and more impressive than the last as you climb to the top. Career progress is measured by classification level, job titles, and how quickly you move from APS to EL and beyond. With this mindset if you are not moving up, it can feel like you are standing still.

Careers are rarely that neat, most APS careers are built through sideways moves, temporary roles, project work, secondments, specialist positions, and periods of consolidation. Depth develops by moving across functions, building knowledge, skills, experience and networks. Credibility is built by stepping into stretch roles even if they aren't promotions. Balance is regained by choosing to consolidate for a defined period of time.

This creates a career that no series of straight-line promotions ever could, it is often far more fulfilling and enjoyable along the way too.

"Progress is not a direction.
It's a series of decisions."

This is why it is more helpful to think about your career as a net rather than a ladder.

In this chapter, we will explore this approach and introduce the five career moves that build successful APS careers. None of them are inherently "better" than the others, each serves a different purpose at different stages.

Understanding these moves will help you recognise opportunities you may currently be overlooking. It will also help you make choices that build long term capability rather than short term status.

Before you think about how to apply, interview, or perform, it is worth getting clear on what your next move is.

Think about career as a net, not a ladder

If we only think about careers as ladders, the only possible moves are up or down. Many APS careers begin in entry level roles or graduate programs within a specific technical field. Over time, people build expertise, perform well and move into more senior technical positions. Eventually, that progression may lead to coordination roles and then into team leadership. While this pathway is common, it is only one way a career can develop.

I encourage you to start thinking about your career as a net rather than a ladder. When careers are viewed as ladders, promotion becomes the main measure of success and anything that is not a move "up" can feel like failure.

A senior leader I once worked with encouraged me to explore roles across different functions earlier in my career. His view was that it becomes harder to move sideways at more senior levels, so building breadth early matters. By working in areas like finance, HR, policy, or technical teams earlier on, people avoided being labelled too narrowly in one field. That broader experience made it much easier for them to step into different opportunities later in their careers.

Sometimes you move for advancement, other times you move to learn something new, to realign with what matters to you, to consolidate your experience, or even to start again.

When you think about your career this way, the focus shifts from chasing the next rung to building capability, confidence, and choice and making conscious choices in your career.

The Five Career Moves

With the net rather than ladder mindset, there are five possible career moves rather than just two you can consider. Each move has a different purpose and presents different opportunities, and risks.

Understanding the different types of career moves helps you make more intentional choices. Not every application needs to be for a promotion however, every application needs preparation, clarity, and respect for the process.

The five moves are:

- Upwards
- Sideways
- Backwards
- Pause, and
- Transformation

Let's explore each one and what they might look like.

The Upwards Move: Stepping Up

This is the move most people think of first. With a promotion comes more responsibility, greater influence, higher expectations and usually better conditions.

Before an upwards move ask yourself:

Am I ready for this level of complexity, autonomy, and leadership?

Am I prepared to take on all of the responsibilities required of someone in this position?

Upwards moves are exciting, they are also demanding and need to be a conscious choice. Accepting not only the benefits and conditions but also the requirements and demands that come with new level.

I've seen many people pursue promotion for the salary or recognition, without considering the full responsibilities of the role, particularly managing staff. The result is often a job they don't enjoy and don't perform strongly in.

Do I have sufficient evidence of my ability at this level?

In the APS, promotion is not based on potential, it is about demonstrated capability at the new level. If you are aiming upwards, your preparation needs to focus on higher level examples, increased strategic thinking, greater autonomy and broader influence.

The Sideways Move: Broadening

Sideways moves happen at the same classification or responsibility level but in a different team, function, agency, or subject matter area.

These moves are often underestimated and are some of the most powerful career builders available. A sideways move can:

- Broaden your skill set
- Build organisational knowledge
- Expand your network
- Expose you to new ways of working

Before a sideways move ask:

What skills, perspectives, or networks will this move help me build that I currently need to develop?

How will this role stretch me beyond my comfort zone?

How does this move strengthen my longer-term career story, even if it does not look like "progress" right now?

Throughout my public service career, I made several sideways moves across IT, HR, change management, and stakeholder engagement roles and across different agencies.

It didn't always look like "progress" however, it gave me depth, flexibility, and perspective that later supported me in leadership roles.

Sideways moves still require strong applications and interviews. Panels want to see how your experience will transfer and why the move makes sense for you and for them.

The Backwards Move: Realigning

Sometimes, the right move is technically a step backwards. There are many potential benefits in moving to a lower classification, a different field, a role with less status but more meaning or flexibility to better integrate work into your life. This is often driven by:

- Values
- Family needs
- Wellbeing
- Long term career redirection
- Stage of life

Before a backwards move ask:

What am I gaining through this move that matters more to me than status or seniority?

How does this role support my wellbeing, values, or life priorities at this stage?

Can I clearly explain how this move strengthens my long-term capability and direction?

One of my own backwards moves was stepping away from full time public service work to become a stay at home dad for six months.

During that time, I also began building my coaching practice and leadership development consultancy. It didn't look like career advancement in the traditional sense and many people thought it was a strange decision. However it was the right choice because it deeply aligned with what mattered most to me at that stage of life and has led to me writing this book. I can't say whether it would exist if I was still working in the APS.

Backwards moves require courage and also a clear narrative. If you're applying for roles that look like backwards moves you need to be able to explain why this move makes sense and how it strengthens, rather than weakens, your long term capability.

The Pause: Consolidating and Strengthening

Not moving can be a powerful move as long as it is intentional. Sometimes, the best decision is to stay where you are and focus on:

- Building depth
- Delivering strong results
- Developing confidence
- Managing life priorities
- Recovering energy

The intentional pause is about consolidation, not stagnation. Many people drift into pauses without choosing them and you want to avoid doing that. Staying in roles too long out of comfort, fear, or habit is not a career move.

I have done this myself because I enjoyed the work or the people I was working with and only realised in hindsight that I should have been more proactive in managing my career and moved earlier. Staying too long meant I missed out on development opportunities, had less challenge in my work and was therefore less fulfilled and made progress less quickly in my career.

A healthy pause must be a conscious pause. This means you know why you are staying, you know what you are building towards and you know when you will review it.

An unhealthy pause means you wake up one morning and ask yourself "how am I still here?" or "Where did everyone else go?"

Before a Pause ask yourself:

Am I staying here by choice, or by default?

What specific capabilities, confidence, or results am I intentionally building during this time?

When and how will I review whether this pause is still serving me?

The Transformation: Starting Again

The fifth move is the most significant move, a complete shift into something new. This might involve:

- Changing professions
- Moving sectors
- Starting a business
- Retraining
- Redefining your identity at work

These moves often feel risky and can involve temporary loss of status, income, or certainty. They also open the door to work that is more aligned, meaningful, and sustainable.

Before a Transformation ask yourself:

What is pulling me towards this new direction, and why now?

What learning, preparation, and experimentation have I done to test this path?

How can I connect my past experience to where I want to go next?

Transformation moves require careful planning because panels and recruiters will want to understand your motivation, your learning journey, and how your experience is relevant. You might have to take small steps towards a larger transformation, or a backwards move first to build a new foundation to launch from.

I've been building my leadership consultancy and working for myself for nearly 10 years and the mix of work I have now is very different to how it started. I am also very conscious about unintentionally falling into an unhealthy pause and remain focussed on continuing to grow and find new ways to challenge myself and continue to do interesting work.

Every Move Still Requires Preparation

Regardless of which move you are making, the recruitment process still matters and you need to prepare for it.

Whatever move you make you are entering a structured system that values evidence, clarity, and alignment.

The mistake many people make is assuming that "non promotion" moves don't require the same level of preparation, they do, in fact sometimes they need more. Panels still ask and you'll need an answer for:

- Why this move?
- Why now?
- Why you?
- What will you bring?

Being clear on your current desired career move helps you answer these questions with confidence and integrity.

Reflection: Naming Your Next Move

Before looking at possible roles, pause and ask yourself, which move am I making right now?

- Upwards
- Sideways
- Backwards
- Pause
- Transformation

Why is this the right move for me at this stage?

What evidence do I need to show to support it?

There is no "right" or "wrong" move. There is only the move that aligns with your values, responsibilities, and aspirations right now.

Careers are complex, priorities shift, life changes and different moves matter more at different times so it can be useful to return to this framework regularly to make sure you haven't fallen into an unintentional pause.

Chapter Summary

Thinking in terms of a career net rather than career ladder gives you more flexibility, more options, and more control. Careers in the APS rarely move in straight lines, most people build capability through a series of sideways moves, development roles, temporary assignments, short term higher duties opportunities, and periods of consolidation, not just promotions.

By understanding the different types of moves available, you are better placed to make deliberate choices rather than reactive ones. Instead of applying for roles simply because they are available, familiar, or seen as "the next step", you can begin asking more useful questions:

What am I trying to build?

What capability do I need next?

What experience will serve me in the long term?

The APS does not evaluate candidates based on vague impressions or potential alone. Panels look for specific behaviours that demonstrate capability at a particular classification level. These behaviours are described through the Integrated

Leadership System (ILS), which outlines expectations for roles across the public service.

In the next chapter, we will explore how APS levels differ, how the Integrated Leadership System works, and how you can use it to develop strong examples. You will also learn how to choose action verbs and language that clearly demonstrate your capability at the level you are applying for to support you in making your planned career move.

CHAPTER 2:
Using the right language

Two people can do the same job, have the same capability, and deliver the same results, yet one is seen as "ready for the next level" while the other is not. Often, the difference is not performance, it is the language they use to describe what they have done and in this chapter, you'll learn how to accurately talk about what you have done.

Small shifts in language change how your experience is perceived, and using the ILS helps you avoid underselling, overselling, or guessing what "good" looks like.

"Your experience only counts if you can explain it."

This chapter unpacks how APS classifications, work level standards, and action focused language shape recruitment decisions. You will learn how to describe your experience in ways that match the level you are targeting, use strong and appropriate action verbs, and show not just what you did, but how you operated. When you understand this, you stop guessing what panels want and start communicating your capability with clarity, confidence, and credibility.

APS Levels: A Brief Explanation

For people who are new to the Australian Public Service, the different classification levels can be confusing at first.

This table has broad descriptions so you can find the right level for you to start with.

APS1 and APS2	These roles are entry level positions focused on learning systems, following established processes, and supporting team operations under close supervision.
APS3 and APS4	These roles involve greater independence and technical skill, with responsibility for delivering defined tasks, solving routine problems, and contributing to team outcomes.

APS5 and APS6	These roles require higher levels of judgement, stakeholder engagement, and accountability, often involving managing complex work, mentoring others, and influencing how work is delivered.
Executive Level roles (EL1 and EL2)	These are leadership positions (people or technical) with responsibility for setting direction, managing people and resources, and shaping programs and policies.
Senior Executive Service roles (SES Band 1 to Band 3)	The most senior levels and focus on whole of organisation leadership, strategic decision making, and accountability to organisation secretaries / CEOs, ministers, and government.

The Integrated Leadership System

The Australian Public Service Commission (APSC) has a range of documents which form the ILS. The APSC says it *"provides capability development guidance for individuals and agencies in the form of descriptions and behaviours for all levels in the APS."*

I say it is underutilised and should form the foundation for your recruitment preparation. You can find it here

https://www.apsc.gov.au/working-aps/hr-practitioners/classification-and-work-level-standards/integrated-leadership-system-ils

or just search for "APSC ILS" in your favourite search engine.

A deeper look at the comparison table

Sometimes it is hard to determine what the differences between levels are, the ILS outlines clear differences in what is required at each level across the public service. Knowing what these differences are and how you need to demonstrate your experience differently for each level will increase your likelihood of success.

Being a fantastic APS5 will not necessarily mean you are found suitable at the APS6 level. The same is true for APS6 to EL1, EL1 to EL2, etc.

The APSC produces a comparison table which shows the difference between expected capabilities and behaviours at different levels. These are in two groups APS1-6 and EL-SES.

You can find the comparison for the level you are currently at / applying for on the APSC website. When you look at these tables you will see the different language used to describe desired behaviours for each level and can adjust your examples to match.

Unfortunately, there isn't a comparison table between APS6 and EL1 produced by the APSC. I have created one that you can access here.

APSrecruitmentgame.com.au

To demonstrate this further, let's look at the differences between APS5 and APS6 for the behaviour "Shows judgement, intelligence and commonsense."

APS5	APS6
Undertakes objective, systematic analysis and draws accurate conclusions based on evidence.	Undertakes objective, systematic analysis and draws accurate conclusions based on evidence. **Recognises the links between interconnected issues.**
Identifies problems and works to resolve them.	Identifies problems and works to resolve them.
Thinks laterally, identifies and implements improved work practices	Thinks laterally, identifies, implements and **promotes** improved work practices.

This table has been sourced from the APSC ILS APS1-6 comparative page, and the differences are displayed in italics and bold as they are there.

If you are applying for a APS5 position you need to demonstrate how you have thought laterally, identified and implemented improved work practices. However, at the APS6 level you will also need to discuss how you promoted them within the relevant work area and how you recognised the links between interconnected issues in your work.

Matching Your Language to Your Level

When you look at the ILS, you will notice a progression in the behaviours as you move up the levels.

At lower levels, the language commonly used is:

- Supports
- Follows direction
- Responds
- Works independently on routine tasks
- Uses own capabilities
- Monitors progress
- Sees tasks through to completion
- Builds and sustains relationships

At middle levels, it shifts to:

- Monitors project progress
- Adjusts plans as required
- Negotiates responsibility
- Identifies opportunities for improvement
- Responds positively to change
- Shares information with others
- Actively listens and consults
- Encourages cooperation
- Demonstrates self-evaluation

At senior levels, the behaviours move to:

- Provides direction
- Translates strategy into operational goals
- Communicates expected outcomes
- Aligns tasks with organisational objectives
- Builds networks and relationships
- Proactively offers assistance
- Encourages and consults stakeholders
- Drives change
- Builds capability
- Governs risk
- Fosters collaboration across business units
- Motivates and empowers teams

Using the ILS to describe what you have done

Once you understand the ILS and how the different levels compare, you can stop guessing how to describe your work and start doing it accurately. For example, you might have: "helped everyone in the team to stay organised."

At the APS5–6 level, that might be described as: "I coordinated workflows and prioritised competing deadlines for my team."

At the EL1 level, it might become: "I established systems to manage team workloads and mitigate delivery risks."

Using precise language to describe your experience helps the panel accurately assess your skills and capability at the level you are applying for.

Why Verbs (Action Words) Matter

The verbs you use need to match with the ILS description for the level you're applying for. If you use verbs that are too junior, you undersell yourself. If you describe using action words that are too senior, you sound unrealistic or disconnected from your actual experience.

Using the ILS helps you land in the right place and avoid three mistakes that are commonly made.

Avoiding Three Common Mistakes

There are three mistakes I see repeatedly in APS recruitment processes. People either are not fully aware of what they've done, undersell what they've done, or oversell what they've done.

When candidates aren't aware of what they've done, they overlook strong examples and provide vague or incomplete responses that don't reflect their true capability. Underselling shows up when people downplay their role or fail to clearly link their actions to outcomes, leaving panels unsure of their contribution. Overselling creates a different issue, where exaggerated or unsupported claims raise doubts about credibility and judgement.

Across all three, the common issue is clarity. Potentially strong candidates are overlooked because they haven't translated their experience in a way that gives the panel confidence.

Let's take a closer look at how each of these mistakes shows up and what to do about them.

Mistake One:
Not Being Aware of What You've Done

The first mistake is not being aware of what you've actually done.

People commonly say to me, "I just do my job" and that might be true, but you do it differently to me and your colleagues. The mistake is that "I just do my job" doesn't help you navigate a recruitment process.

Panels are not assessing effort or good intentions; they are assessing evidence of behaviour and capability. If you cannot clearly explain what you did, the impact it had, and how you approached the work, the panel has nothing to assess.

Often this lack of awareness happens because the work feels normal to you. You've been doing it for months or years and it no longer feels remarkable. But work that feels routine to you needs to demonstrate capability and expertise at the level you are applying for.

The first step is pausing to reflect so you can recognise the capability you already demonstrate, we'll explore that shortly.

Mistake Two:
Underselling Your Contribution

The second mistake is underselling. Highly capable people, especially in technical or specialist roles, often describe senior level work using very modest language. They say they "helped", "assisted", or "supported" when in reality they "led", "designed", or "drove outcomes".

Panels need to understand your contribution. If everything is described as helping or supporting, it becomes difficult for them to see your decision making, leadership, or influence.

People often tell me in career coaching sessions that they worry about being arrogant. People who are genuinely concerned about this rarely do and those who come across as arrogant don't think about how they sound at all, as far as I can tell.

Being clear about your role, effort and outcomes is not arrogance, it is simply giving the panel accurate information about the work you did.

So, focus on being clear, confident and accurate in how you describe what you have done.

Mistake Three:
Overselling Your Contribution

The third mistake is overselling. Sometimes candidates go in the opposite direction and describe their work using language that suggests a much higher level of responsibility than they held.

Panels notice this quickly as you are unable to explain or justify your use of that language.

For example, someone might say they "led a major strategic initiative" when in reality they contributed to a piece of work within a larger project. When the panel explores the example further, the gap becomes obvious and this damages credibility. The panel begins to question whether the candidate fully understands the expectations of the level they are applying for and whether they are a good fit for the role. If they are prepared to oversell this what else might they be overselling.

One of the most useful tools for getting this balance right is the Integrated Leadership System (ILS). It provides a clear description of the behaviours expected at each APS level. When you understand how the ILS works, it becomes much easier to recognise the level of work you have been doing and to describe it in a way that is accurate and aligned with the role you are applying for.

In the next section, we'll look more closely at how the ILS is structured and how you can use it to develop stronger examples and use language that reflects the level of responsibility you've held.

Reflection: ILS Self Assessment Checklists

The ILS includes self assessment checklists for APS1 through SESB3 levels that give a detailed description and outline the expected behaviours of someone operating at each level. I recommend grabbing a cup of tea or coffee and a quiet space to review both the Self Assessment Checklist for your current and aspirational level/s (if different) and the Comparison Table over the next few days.

Using this you can develop a set of examples by identifying which example you would provide to demonstrate each behaviour.

This will take time to work through and you want to make sure you are not just ticking the box but thinking about the STAR example (see chapter 5) you would provide for each behaviour. When you don't have an example that might be a potential development opportunity which you could discuss with your manager.

Chapter Summary

The Integrated Leadership System (ILS) removes much of the mystery from APS recruitment. It shows you, in plain language, how people at different levels are expected to think, decide, lead, engage and deliver. When you use it well, you stop relying on instinct or hope and start positioning yourself with clarity and accuracy.

By working through the self assessment checklists, studying the comparison tables, and adjusting your language deliberately, you give panels what they are actually looking for. Evidence that you understand the level you are applying for and can operate effectively within it. You also protect yourself from the traps of not knowing how you do your job, underselling your contribution and overstating your role. You'll have a professional vocabulary for what you do every day and a framework for planning your next steps.

In Chapter 3, we shift from capability and classification to fit, using a practical framework to help you choose roles that align with your strengths, aspirations, and life.

CHAPTER 3:
Finding the right job

Before you worry about applying for a job, make sure it's one you actually want.

Too often, people rush this step and apply broadly in the hope that something, anything, will stick. It might be to escape a current role or reach the next level. The problem is, when the role isn't a good fit, even success can feel hollow and before long you are back in the recruitment process looking for something better.

When you choose the right roles, everything improves. You write stronger applications, perform better in interviews, and present with more confidence. A more intentional approach focuses your energy where it matters and sets you up to perform at your best.

This chapter starts by showing you how to read APS job advertisements properly, including how to interpret essential and desirable criteria and what panels are really signalling through their language. From there, it introduces the Three Fits Framework, a practical way to assess whether a role aligns with the work you want to do, the level you want to operate at, and the life you want to live.

It is easy to talk yourself into applying for roles based on status, security, timing, or other people's expectations. It is much harder, and far more valuable, to pause and ask whether a role genuinely fits who you are and how you want to work. When you do this well, you stop applying reactively and start choosing strategically.

"Guessing is expensive.
Preparation is an investment."

Most APS job advertisements are dense and easy to skim, which means important details that should shape your approach are often missed. Faced with pages of criteria, capability statements and organisational context, many candidates jump straight into drafting just to feel like they are making progress.

In doing so, they overlook what matters most. They have not stepped back to consider whether the role is the right fit, whether it offers the right level of challenge, or whether it aligns with their lifestyle. Ultimately, they have not decided if it is the right job for them and whether they should even be applying.

Before you think about examples, resumes, or interview answers, slow down and properly unpack the job ad. It is not just an administrative document. It reflects the team's priorities, pressures, and expectations. The description shows where the role sits, the duties reveal what will take up your time, and the criteria highlight what the panel will assess.

Pay attention to repeated words, key themes, and the balance between technical, strategic, and people focused language. Notice what is emphasised and what is not.

When you read job ads this way, you move from passively responding to actively interpreting, and that gives you a real advantage before you even begin your application.

Reading the job advertisement

It's worth slowing down and properly analysing the job advertisement. By correctly interpreting different types of criteria, understanding what is truly non negotiable, recognising where there is more flexibility and reading between the lines of the "successful candidate" section, you can spot what matters most to the panel right now. Done well, this helps you focus your effort where it will have the greatest impact.

Understanding different criteria types

Almost every APS job advertisement includes a section that begins with some version of:

"As the successful candidate, you will bring…" or

"The key duties of the position include:"

Underneath this, you will usually see a list of:

- Essential criteria
- Desirable criteria
- Capabilities
- Qualifications
- Experience requirements

This section is one of the most important parts of the job ad. It is where the panel tells you, as clearly as they can, what they are looking for.

Learning how to read it well will save you time, energy, and reduce ultimately unnecessary self doubt.

Essential Criteria: What Is Non Negotiable

Some essential criteria really are essential. For example, legal, professional, or regulatory requirements that people in the role need to meet. Examples include:

- CPA or CA qualifications for finance roles
- Law degrees and admission requirements for legal roles
- Professional registration in specialist fields
- Citizenship or
- Ability to pass a Police Check

If you do not meet these, you are unlikely to progress. No amount of well written selection criteria and strong interviewing will compensate for missing mandatory requirements.

This is not unfair, it reflects the real constraints of the role and expectations of the person in it.

If you are expected to obtain and/or maintain a security clearance, pass a health or police check then you'll be given information on how to do this by the recruitment team at the appropriate time.

When "Essential" Is More Flexible

However, many "essential" criteria are not as rigid as they appear. They often relate to:

- Experience in a particular area
- Familiarity with certain systems
- Exposure to specific policy environments
- Understanding of processes, frameworks or legislation

In practice, panels are often assessing *Can this person do the job with reasonable support?"* Not *"Have they done this exact job before?"*

Desirable Criteria: Guides, not rules

Desirable criteria indicate what would be helpful, not what is required. They are used to:

- Differentiate strong candidates
- Highlight preferred backgrounds
- Indicate future direction

Being unable to demonstrate how you meet a desirable criteria rarely rules you out immediately, you should focus on showing your other relevant strengths to overcome it though.

"Working Towards" and "Ability to Acquire"

Many ads include phrases like:

- "Working towards…"
- "Ability to quickly acquire…"
- "Willingness to undertake…"
- "Capacity to develop…"

They are saying *"we know not everyone will have this yet."* So please do not automatically exclude yourself when you see these. Instead, ask, *"How can I show that I'm capable of getting there?"*

Turning Gaps into Strengths

If you are missing something that is described as "working towards" or "ability to acquire", address it directly. In your resume or selection criteria, you might include any:

- Current study to build your knowledge
- Planned training to gain skills
- Relevant experience in similar areas
- Self directed learning that you have completed
- Past examples of rapid skill development

For example:

"I am currently enrolled in…"

"I have begun developing capability in…"

"In previous roles, I quickly built expertise in…"

This shows initiative, credibility and self awareness. It also shows the panel that you have thought about your self in the role and what you would bring to it.

Reading Between the Lines

The "successful candidate" section often reflects:

- Immediate pressures in the team
- Skill shortages
- Upcoming projects
- Leadership priorities

So, matching your experience to these can help the panel determine how quickly you would be able to help them overcome the challenges and exploit the opportunities that the team and/or organisation are facing at the moment.

Deliberately Match Your Evidence

For every criteria, think of an example of something that you have done that shows:

- Where you have done this
- How well you did it
- What you learned
- How it applies here

Once you understand how to read a job advertisement and interpret its essential and desirable criteria, you can see what really matters to the panel, where you are a strong match, and where you may need to strengthen your examples.

After unpacking what the role is about, the next step is to turn that outward analysis inward. Understanding the job description tells you what the organisation needs, the Three Fits Framework helps you decide whether those needs align with who you are, how you work and where you are in your life right now.

This is where the question shifts from *"Can I do this job?"* to *"Is this the right job for me at this point in my career?"*

By considering Content Fit, Challenge Fit and Lifestyle Fit alongside what the advertisement is signalling, you move from reacting to advertisements to seeking out and choosing options deliberately. Instead of applying because you feel pressure, urgency or momentum, you choose with clarity and intent.

The Three Fits Framework

The Three Fits framework is designed to create clarity on whether the job you are applying for is right for you, at this particular time. It invites you to consider Content Fit, Challenge Fit and Lifestyle Fit before you apply. Acknowledging that careers are complex and rarely neat, there will be times when one fit matters more than the others, and that's okay.

I believe you're allowed to be selfish in your career choices. Looking out for what matters to you isn't indulgent, it's responsible. Noting, that what's best for you needs to work for the people around you too so you'll need to consider that. When a role aligns with what you value, how you want to work and where you are in your life, you're far more likely to show up calm, confident and capable not only during recruitment but in the role as well.

Let's take a more intentional approach using the Three Fits Framework, use these questions as your starting point.

Download a copy of this worksheet at
apsrecruitmentgame.com.au

Content Fit

How excited about the work am I?

How does this role give me opportunities to use my strengths?

Would I enjoy doing this most days?

How does the work of the organisation align with my values?

How would I explain my understanding of the role to a friend.

Challenge Fit

Use the Integrated Leadership System (ILS) to check whether the role matches your:

- broad work expectations
- expected amount of autonomy
- desired leadership responsibilities
- decision making scope

Are these aligned to where I can and want to operate?

Is the level of challenge at the right level or is it too high or too low?

Lifestyle Fit

Think about flexibility, workload, subject matter, hybrid work and any travel requirements or unpredictable peaks.

Are there restrictions around work from home or work patterns (shift work or on call) that I need to consider?

Can I picture myself thriving in this environment?

Will I be thinking about work when I'm not there and what impact will that have on my life?

Score Each Fit Area

Give each fit a score from 1 to 5, there are no "right" or "wrong" answers.

Lower scores could be for levels being too low or too high. I.e. there might not be enough responsibility or there could be too much.

1 = Very Low Fit

Significant mismatch. This role would likely be frustrating, stressful, or unsustainable.

2 = Low Fit

Some alignment, but major gaps or concerns.

3 = Moderate Fit

Reasonable alignment, with clear strengths and limitations.

4 = High Fit

Strong alignment. Most elements suit you well.

5 = Excellent Fit

Outstanding alignment. This role strongly matches who you are and what you want.

Reflection: Plot Your Three Fits Scores

Transfer your three scores onto the Three Fits triangle. Each side of the triangle represents one dimension:

- Content Fit
- Challenge Fit
- Lifestyle Fit

Join your three scores to create a triangle and colour it in. We'll interpret what the results mean over the next few pages.

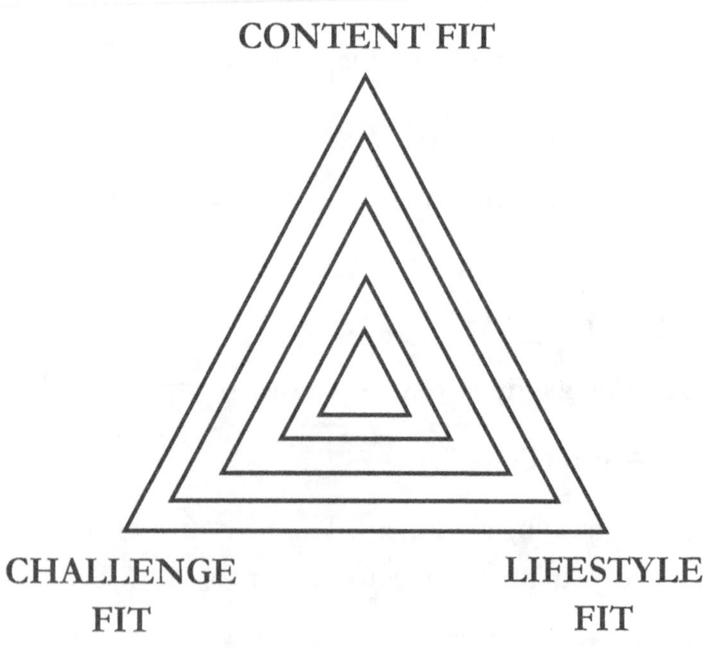

Interpreting Your Triangle

Once you have plotted your scores, reflect on the overall shape.

Balanced and Full Triangle

High scores across all three dimensions suggest strong alignment. These roles are usually sustainable, motivating, and developmentally healthy and you are likely to enjoy working in it if you were successful in your application.

Strong in Two Areas, Weak in One

This is common, ask yourself:

- Is the weaker area temporary or ongoing?
- Can it be managed, negotiated, or supported?
- Am I willing to accept this trade-off right now

I've explored some common experiences of different combinations of two strong areas and one weak one below.

Example 1: High Content Fit, High Challenge Fit, Low Lifestyle Fit

What This Looks Like in Practice

This person loves the work and feels capable with the level of challenge. They are intellectually engaged and respected by colleagues. However, the hours are long, travel is frequent, or workloads are unpredictable.

Over time, they may feel constantly tired, stretched between work and personal life, and emotionally depleted. They often say things like, "I love my job, but it's exhausting." Without changes, burnout becomes a real risk because of the lifestyle impact.

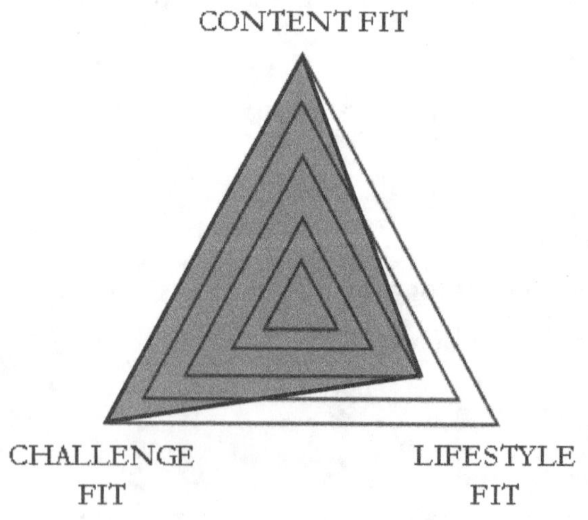

Example 2: High Content Fit, High Lifestyle Fit, Low Challenge Fit

What This Looks Like in Practice

The work is meaningful and the conditions are supportive. The person has flexibility, reasonable hours, and time for life outside of work. However, the level of challenge does not match their capability by either being too high or too low.

They may feel underutilised, frustrated, or invisible and after an initial settling period, boredom creeps in. Or they may be overwhelmed and responsible for more than they're ready to be accountable for.

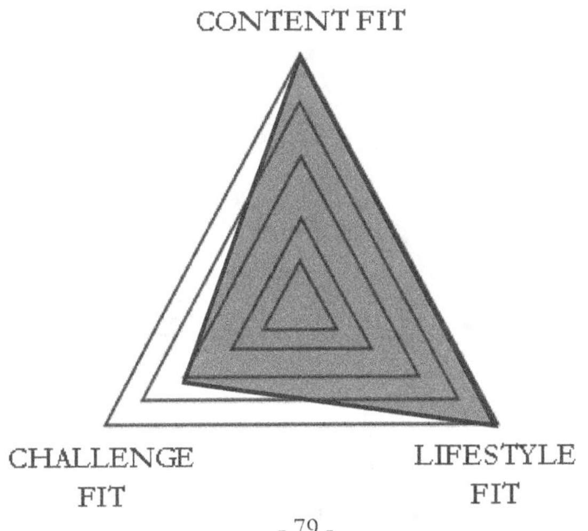

Example 3: High Challenge Fit, High Lifestyle Fit, Low Content Fit

What This Looks Like in Practice

This person operates comfortably with the level of challenge and enjoys good working conditions. They are trusted, autonomous, and well supported. On paper, the job looks ideal.

The problem is that the work itself does not interest them, they feel emotionally detached and disengaged. Over time, motivation drops and performance can flatten. They often describe feeling "stuck" or "uninspired" or say I'm here for the money but they don't enjoy their time at work.

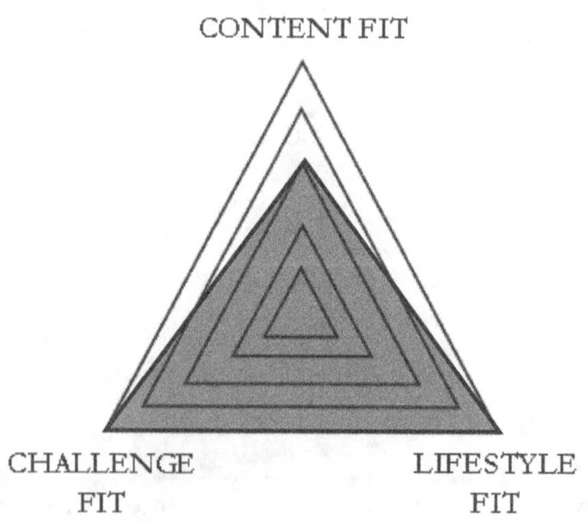

One Very Low Score

A score of 1 or 2 in any dimension is a warning sign. Over time, low fit in one area often undermines the others and makes it hard for you to remain motivated in the role. You should think about whether this is the right role for you or whether you should continue to look for a better fit.

Small Overall Triangle

Low scores across all areas suggest the role is unlikely to be good for you. So strongly consider whether this is the right role for you to apply for. Engaging in recruitment processes takes a lot of energy and time so decide whether this is the best one for you to be investing in.

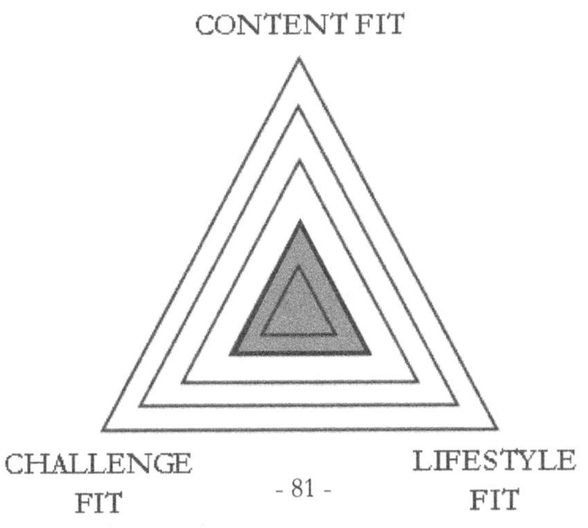

Reflection: Your Last Three Roles

Thinking about your last three jobs or applications

Which of the three fits were strong?

What made them strong?

What was the impact on your level of engagement?

Which of the three fits were weakest?

What made them weak?

What was the impact on your level of engagement?

Inside the Interview Room

I was on a recruitment panel for an EL1 leadership role in a highly technical environment. Early in the interview it became clear that the applicant didn't have a strong grasp of the actual role requirements. When asked leadership focused questions, they consistently responded by talking about their technical expertise rather than demonstrating how they led people or made decisions at the EL1 level.

There was also very little evidence that they understood the work of the department or how the role contributed to the broader organisational context. The disconnect was confirmed at the end of the interview when the panel invited questions and the applicant asked, *"Did I actually apply for this job?"* It was a moment of awkward honesty, but it confirmed what the panel was already thinking.

Unsurprisingly, the applicant was found not suitable because they did not demonstrate the required leadership capability. They had not taken the time to understand whether the role was the right fit for them and how to properly present their skills.

You have now learned how to unpack a job advertisement so you can clearly understand what the organisation is actually looking for. Instead of skimming the criteria, you can interpret the signals in the advertisement and identify what really matters to the panel.

You have also applied the Three Fits Framework to test whether a role makes sense for you in terms of content, level, and lifestyle, and how that aligns with where you are in your career and life right now.

This puts you in a much stronger position. Rather than applying on instinct, urgency, or frustration, you are making more deliberate choices about where to focus your energy and effort. You are choosing roles that genuinely make sense for you.

The next step is learning how to use AI as a practical support tool to strengthen this thinking. Used well, it can help you analyse job requirements, sharpen your focus, and prepare more effectively, while still ensuring your application reflects your own experience, judgement, and voice.

Using AI to Support Your Job Search

Artificial intelligence tools are now part of everyday work and applicants are using them to support job searching, application writing, and preparation.

Used well, AI can be a helpful thinking partner. Used poorly, it can weaken your application and create real risks.

Using AI as a Second Pair of Eyes

One of the most effective uses of AI is as a reviewer. You can ask it to:

- Summarise key requirements
- Identify recurring themes
- Highlight capability expectations
- Compare your experience with role requirements
- Flag potential gaps

For example:

"What are five important capabilities in this role?"

This helps you focus your preparation however it does not replace careful reading. It helps you notice patterns you may miss when tired or under pressure.

Analysing Job Fit

AI can support reflection on whether a role suits you. You might ask:

"How well does my experience align with this role?"

"Where are my strongest matches?"

"Where am I weakest and I need to improve?"

This provides another perspective to inform your decision making. Treat it as input, not truth.

AI can and will get things wrong; make sure you thoroughly check everything it produces.

You remain responsible for the final submission.

Identifying Key Themes and Language

You can use AI and online tools to analyse language in job advertisements and selection criteria.

Word clouds and theme analysis highlight what appears most often and can help you focus or tighten your responses.

If a role emphasises stakeholder engagement, governance, and delivery, but your experience is in other areas, that is useful information. It does not mean you are unsuitable, it means you may need to adjust your examples and language.

Testing Draft Applications

AI can review draft responses before submission. You might ask:

"Does this address the criteria clearly?"

"Where could this be more specific?"

"Is this pitched at the (appropriate ILS) level?"

This helps tighten your writing and reduce avoidable weaknesses, which you can address before you submit it for consideration.

Privacy, Accuracy, and Responsibility

Again, you are responsible for anything you upload. Do not share:

- Sensitive government information
- Classified material
- Confidential project details
- Personal data without consent

Never Blindly Trust AI Output

AI systems can:

- Be wrong
- Misinterpret context
- Invent information or hallucinate
- Oversimplify complex roles
- Reflect bias in their training data

So, use it to support you but do not just upload what it produces without analysing it.

Chapter Summary

Finding the right role should not be about chasing prestige, security, or what looks good on paper, you need to understand yourself and make deliberate choices. The Three Fits Framework gives you a simple way to determine whether a role aligns with your desired content, level and lifestyle mix.

When you are clear about fit, everything else becomes easier. Your applications are more focused, your interview responses are more grounded and your performance is more authentic. You don't need to convince yourself or others that a match will work out, you are clear on how good a match you are.

You are no longer relying on guesswork or assumptions. You have done the quiet, disciplined work of analysis and reflection. But even the best written job ad and the smartest tools cannot tell you everything. Every role sits inside a real team, with real pressures, priorities, and expectations that are not always visible on paper. To understand those, you need to move from analysis to conversation, it's time to call the contact officer.

CHAPTER 4:
The contact officer

Most applicants treat the contact officer as a last resort, I want you to treat them as a strategic ally.

Reaching out to the contact officer can feel awkward, unnecessary, or even risky. People worry they'll say the wrong thing, that they're bothering someone who is already busy or assume the advertisement tells them what they need to know.

Talking to the contact officer is a valuable part of the process because it gives you context that no document can completely capture which informs your decision of whether the role is right for you, before you invest your time and energy in applying for the job.

This isn't about trying to get an advantage or being remembered, the contact officer may not even be a member of the panel. It's about you better understanding the work, the expectations and the environment so you can apply with clarity rather than guesswork.

Why you should talk to the Contact Officer

A short conversation with the contact officer can help you understand:

- what the team is focused on right now,
- how success is defined in the role,
- what the biggest challenges are, and
- how well the role aligns with your skills and interests.

"Careers are built one well prepared conversation at a time."

This should shape everything that follows, from how you frame your examples to whether you apply at all.

What the Call Is and Isn't

It's worth being clear about your intention for this call. Think of it as:

- a fact finding conversation,
- a chance to test your understanding of the role,
- an opportunity to decide if this role is a good fit for you.

The call is not:

- an informal interview,
- just a pitch about how great you are,
- a chance to ask about salary, leave or conditions, (you can find these answers online),
- a shortcut through the process.

Keeping this in mind takes the pressure off because you don't need to perform, you just need to have a few thoughtful questions to ask, be professional and friendly.

It's useful to have a quick overview of your skills and experience ready as you may be asked. Reading through the rest of the book will help you distil what will be useful to share if you're asked while talking to the contact officer.

A Note on Confidence

You don't need to sound polished and you don't need perfect questions. Contact officers are usually generous with their time and appreciative of applicants who are thoughtful and show that they have put some effort into preparing for the conversation. If they don't behave this way then that's information for you about the organisation and team, which informs your decision on whether you want to work there.

If it helps, you can even name your intention:

> *I'm considering applying and wanted to check my understanding of the role before I do.*

That simple framing at the start lowers the stakes for everyone.

Tip: Download and save the Position Description and related documents

These documents can be useful to refer to throughout the process and are typically not available once applications close.

If you decide after this conversation to continue with your application then download a copy and keep it on hand so that you can continue to refer to it throughout the recruitment process.

When to Reach Out

Ideally, reach out early, before you start writing, this gives you time to reflect on what you hear and adjust your approach.

If you're applying close to the deadline, even a short discussion can be helpful because a quick clarification is better than none.

Three Questions That Almost Always Help

You don't need a long list of things to talk about. Two or three well chosen questions are enough.

1. **What are the top priorities for this role in the next three to six months?**

This tells you what matters most right now, not just in theory. Make sure you've had a look at the organisations' website and read through any strategies and census results that are available. At more senior levels it can be useful to demonstrate your awareness of these documents in your question.

I saw the People Capability Strategy on the website and think Focus Area 1 is relevant to this role, can you outline how the team is delivering against that to me?

2. **What does success look like for someone in this role?**

This helps you shape your examples around impact, not tasks. You can align your examples and achievements more closely with what success looks like for this particular role.

3. **What skills or behaviours tend to identify strong candidates at this level in your team?**

This helps you understand how capability is interpreted locally, not just in the ILS.

Using What You Learn from the contact officer

After the call pause and ask yourself:

- does this role still excite me?
- do I have examples that match what they described?
- do any of the Three Fits feel stronger or weaker?
- What impact does that have on my desire to apply?

Reflection: Calling Contact Officers

What holds you back from calling contact officers?

What would help you feel more confident?

Inside the Interview Room

While I was looking for a new role I saw a job that could be a good next step. On first scan, the job looked like a strong Three Fits match. However, the advertisement included several acronyms I didn't recognise and a handful of Essential Capabilities I wasn't sure I met.

Rather than ruling myself out, I called the contact officer to clarify my understanding of the role. In that short conversation, it became clear that the acronyms were simply internal language for tasks I was very capable of doing. The capabilities that gave me pause were skills the team expected someone to develop on the job, not arrive with fully formed.

That call changed everything. I applied, was successful, and went on to spend two rewarding and productive years in the role. It's a simple example, but a powerful reminder that without that conversation I would likely have talked myself out of an opportunity that turned out to be a great fit.

Worksheet: The Contact Officer Call

"Hi, my name is ________________________________

I'm considering applying and wanted to check my understanding of the role before I do."

Role:	
Agency:	
Questions I'll ask: Feel free to add your own.	What are the top priorities for this role in the next three to six months? What does success look like for someone in this role? This helps you shape your examples around impact, not tasks. What skills or behaviours tend to identify strong candidates at this level in your team?
Notes:	

Download a copy of this worksheet at
apsrecruitmentgame.com.au

Chapter Summary

Speaking with the contact officer is one of the simplest ways to improve the quality of your job search. It gives you insight into priorities, pressures, and expectations that no advertisement can convey. Importantly, it helps you test whether a role genuinely aligns with your skills, interests, and stage of life before you commit to the application process.

When you approach these conversations with curiosity rather than a need to perform, they become a powerful source of clarity and confidence.

Over time, this changes how you apply. You engage with opportunities as an informed professional, not just hoping to be selected.

In Chapter 5, we turn to the practical task of writing your application. We will bring together the insights from the Three Fits Framework, the Integrated Leadership System, and your contact officer conversations to help you craft applications that are focused, credible, and aligned to what panels are really assessing.

CHAPTER 5:
Writing your application

When writing your application your focus should not be on just selling yourself, it is about clearly and truthfully articulating your skills, knowledge and experience. In this chapter, we turn all your insight into action. You have reflected on fit, learned the language of the ILS, and gathered context from the contact officer. Now it is time to translate all of that into a strong application. We will explore the difference between pitches and selection criteria, show you how to use STAR and STAR + to clearly present your experience, and introduce practical tools like the seesaw to balance teamwork and personal contribution.

"Panels don't select from potential.
They select from evidence."

By the end of this chapter, you will have a reliable way to turn your experience into structured, credible evidence that panels can easily assess.

Pitch or Selection Criteria

Candidates are often now being asked to submit a short pitch of 500 to 1,000 words or 1 to 2 pages instead of responding to detailed selection criteria.

The APSC describes a pitch as *"a chance to tell the agency why you are the right person for the job."* It should explain why you want the role, why you are interested in the organisation, what you bring, and how your skills, knowledge, experience, and qualifications apply. In simple terms, it answers one central question: Why should we hire you?

A well structured pitch usually includes:

- A clear opening that outlines your interest and briefly summarises your career
- Several thematic paragraphs that showcase key capabilities, each supported by concrete examples
- A closing section that reinforces your motivation and overall fit

A pitch is more narrative and persuasive than selection criteria. It is your opportunity to weave your experience, motivation, values, and strengths into a coherent story. Rather than responding point by point, you are showing how everything fits together and why you make sense for this role, in this organisation, at this time.

Selection criteria are primarily about evidence, they are usually structured around headings, with separate examples showing how you meet them.

Panels are looking for proof that you already have the capabilities they need. The APSC provides guidance that *"agencies may ask you to separately address a number of criteria or to write one general statement expressing your claims for the job"* and *"You should respond to each criterion and, following any guidance in the information pack, explain how you have demonstrated the particular skill or quality.*

https://www.apsc.gov.au/working-aps/joining-aps/cracking-code/3-applying-aps-job-cracking-code

My first APS job had 6 Selection Criterion each with multiple sub Selection Criteria and the application ended up being 41 A4 pages long. It was exhausting to write, and I can only imagine how painful it was for the panel to read all the submissions. To make it worse I didn't get through to interview and had to wait for the next process to apply again.

Shorter pitches are better for everyone, even if it is still frustrating that job advertisements often run well beyond the word limit that they give you explaining the role requirements and ideal candidate.

Whether you are writing a pitch or responding to selection criteria, your claims still need to be supported by strong, well chosen examples. The APSC recommends you *"provide relevant examples from your work, study or community roles. Be clear and to the point. It is important to provide evidence to back up your claims. Where possible use actual, specific examples of what you have done, how well you did it, what you achieved, and how it relates to the requirements of the job."* Frameworks like STAR and STAR+ will help you to do that and we will cover them shortly.

Before we do, there is another important question to consider, which examples should you be using and does it matter if they're recent or older?

Should I Use Recent or Older Examples?

Unfortunately, the honest answer is it depends on the panel.

I've sat on panels where candidates used mostly recent examples and panel members said, *"How good is it that they have such current, up-to-date experience."* On other panels, the same pattern prompted a different reaction: *"They only seem to have recent examples. I'm not sure they have the depth of experience we need."*

I've also seen the opposite; some candidates relied mainly on older examples that were highly relevant and well evidenced. One panel responded with, *"They clearly have a strong history and breadth of experience."* Another said, *"They haven't done much like what we need recently. Are their skills still current?"*

Different panel members value different things, some prioritise currency and recent exposure while others prioritise depth, patterns, and long term capability. Most are looking for some combination of both so the safest approach is not to choose one over the other but to aim for a mix.

Where possible:

- Include at least one or two strong recent examples that show you have current skills
- Include older examples to demonstrate depth, complexity, or sustained capability

A well chosen example from five years ago that closely matches the role will usually be more powerful than a recent example that only partially fits. Equally, a strong recent example reassures the panel that your skills are active and up to date.

Your guiding principle should be quality and relevance, not just timing.

Ask yourself:

- Does this example clearly demonstrate the capability being assessed?
- Does it show appropriate complexity for the level I'm applying for?
- Can I explain it confidently and in detail?

If the answers are yes, it is probably worth using, whether it happened last year or several years ago.

Of course, if you identify that lots of your examples happened years ago you could intentionally take on new tasks in your current role that will help you freshen your examples.

Sometimes, a discussion with your manager will result in them providing context of where you already are completing activities that would be a good example. Or they may have a new piece of work that they can give you that meets your requirements.

Now that you know what format you need to align with, which examples you are using and what language to use to explain what you have done, let's look at how you should structure your writing.

The **STAR** method

STAR helps you provide what panels need using a clear structure. Panels are looking for behavioural evidence, not vague descriptions or general statements about what you might have done.

It also makes your job easier, and in many cases, it is explicitly requested in the application instructions. You are being shown the rules of the game, so if you want to more likely to succeed, follow them.

S is for Situation.

This is where you set the scene, keep it short, think of it as giving the panel just enough context to understand what was happening. Where were you working? What level were you? What was the environment like? What was the problem or opportunity?

T is for Task.

This is your role in the situation. This is the part candidates often either rush or over explain, so aim for clarity rather than detail. What were you responsible for? What did you need to achieve? What outcome were you aiming for?

A is for Action.

This is the heart of your answer, the panel want to know what you actually did. Not the team, not the broader project, not your manager. You. Show your individual contribution while still acknowledging collaboration where it matters. An easy way to do this it to use the seesaw. As quick detour to "The Seesaw" and then we'll look at R for Result.

The Seesaw

The seesaw is a simple way to balance how you talk about your contribution while still acknowledging how you worked with others. In APS recruitment, panels want to understand both. They want to see that you collaborate well, but they also need to clearly identify what *you* did. If you lean too far to one side, the whole answer becomes unbalanced.

Picture a playground seesaw, on one seat you have I, and on the other you have we/ them/ they/ my manager/ the stakeholders, etc. A strong STAR example moves gently between the two so the panel can see the team context without losing sight of your actions.

If you spend the whole answer saying we, the panel struggles to see your capability.

For example:

We developed a new process, we improved the workflow and we delivered the report on time.

This tells the panel almost nothing about what you personally did. You were involved, but how?

On the other hand, some people lean too far into I, which can make them sound disconnected from their colleagues:

I redesigned the process, I fixed the workflow and I delivered the report.

That might be true, but in a public service environment where teamwork is essential, it can come across as lacking awareness of others.

A balanced seesaw might sound like this:

Our team was asked to streamline a slow monthly reporting process. I took the lead by mapping the key steps, identifying the bottlenecks and consulted with two senior analysts to understand where the delays were happening. I then drafted a new workflow and worked with the team to test it over a cycle. Together we refined the steps, which meant that by the next month we reduced the turnaround time from ten days to four.

See how that moves between both sides of the seesaw. The team context is clear, and your contribution is unmistakable.

Here is another example using a Productive Working Relationships situation:

Our section was preparing a briefing pack for an urgent Senate Estimates request. My role was to coordinate three contributors and ensure the information was consistent. I set up a quick check in, clarified expectations and supported one colleague who was unsure about what level of detail was needed. As a team we delivered the pack ahead of the deadline, and the branch head specifically thanked me for keeping everyone aligned under pressure.

Again, the seesaw stays in balance. You show teamwork without disappearing inside it, and you show ownership without taking all the oxygen.

When you write or speak your STAR examples, imagine that seesaw. If it tips too far to one side, gently bring it back by adding either a sentence about your own actions or a sentence about how you worked with or supported others. This tiny shift makes your examples more complete, more assessable and far more persuasive.

R is for Result.

This is the outcome of your actions. What changed or improved? What did you deliver? What feedback did you receive? Strong results show the impact of your actions. Panels want to see the difference you made, even if only in small ways.

Used well, STAR and The Seesaw turn your experience into clear, assessable evidence. They show the panel you understand your own contribution and can speak to your work with confidence. When used consistently it strengthens both your written applications and your interview answers.

STAR sentence starters

When I was learning how to answer questions using STAR, I used the words to start my sentences to get used to the pattern and rhythm.

The situation was…

The task I identified…

The actions I took…

The results were…

This reads and sounds a bit formulaic so you can start in other ways. Some examples are below but feel free to use your own.

Note: make sure you match the words with the level you are applying for. These examples have been aligned in suggested order from early career to more senior roles but draw on the ILS and the Action Verbs section on page 52 for more comprehensive guidance.

Situation: Setting the Context

- In my previous role, I was working on…
- This came up when our team was…
- At the time, we were dealing with…
- I was part of a team that was responsible for…
- This happened during a period when…
- In my role as [position], I was involved in…
- When I was working in [team] at [organisation]…
- The context for this was…

Task: Clarifying Your Responsibility

- I was asked to…
- I was allocated responsibility for…
- My role was to support…
- I was responsible for…
- I was specifically accountable for…
- I led the work on…
- I took responsibility for…
- I took ownership of…
- I was ultimately accountable for…

Action: Showing What You Actually Did

- The first thing I did was…
- I then worked with…
- I made a decision to…
- I approached this by…
- I consulted with…
- I analysed…
- I implemented…
- I adjusted my approach when…
- I deliberately chose to…

Result: Demonstrating Impact

- This led to…
- The outcome was…
- Because of this…
- We were able to…
- This achieved…
- The final impact was…
- This meant that…

STAR +

Sometimes a standard STAR answer is all you need. Clear context, your actions and a solid result will be enough in most APS interviews. But there are moments when going a little deeper helps the panel to see not just what you did, but how you think, what you value and how your experience connects to the role you want next. That's where STAR + comes in.

STAR + contains four optional elements you can weave in when they genuinely strengthen your example. Please don't use all of them every time. Think of them like seasoning, a little at the right moment will lift your answer, too much will spoil the effect.

S is for Strategic Impact

This is where you zoom out for a moment. After sharing your STAR example, you explain how your actions supported a broader goal. Maybe your work contributed to a division priority, an agency reform, a service improvement or an APS wide expectation like collaboration or value like stewardship.

For example, you might say, *This helped the branch meet its commitment to improving data reliability for our external stakeholders as outlined in our Division Plan's KPIs.*

This shows maturity and awareness beyond your immediate task.

T is for Thinking

Panels want to understand the judgement behind your actions. This is a chance to briefly talk through the choices you made. What options did you weigh up? What risks did you consider? Why did you approach the situation the way you did?

This doesn't mean narrating your every thought, it's simply giving a quick window into your reasoning, which is especially helpful at EL1/EL2 and above levels where judgement is heavily assessed. For example, you might say, *In deciding how to approach this, I considered two options. I chose option one after consulting key stakeholders and reviewing the relevant policy guidance, as it provided a more sustainable outcome.*

A is for Applicability

This is especially valuable if you're changing agencies, applying for a different type of role or stepping up a level. Here you connect the dots for the panel. At the end of your STAR answer you might say, *I would use the stakeholder management and prioritisation skills I've outlined in that example in this project coordination role to keep the project on scope, on time and on budget by keeping stakeholders informed and focusing on high priority tasks through regular reporting and discussions with my manager.*

It reassures the panel that your skills transfer even if your past work looks different on paper.

R is for Reflection

Reflection shows awareness and growth, a simple line about what you'd do differently or what you learned can add real depth to your answer. It signals self awareness, adaptability and maturity.

For example, *If I faced the same situation again, I'd bring the key stakeholder in earlier because that would have saved time later.*

Panels appreciate this because it shows you're someone who learns, not just someone who executes.

When used well, STAR + helps you turn a good example into an excellent one. It lets the panel see not just what happened, but how you operate as a professional. Having this in your back pocket gives you more flexibility to show the full picture of your capability when it matters most.

Your Application: The little things matter

When writing your application you follow all the instructions. If the advertisement says to use Arial size 11 font, you use it. Yes, even if you like Calibri size 13 more. If it says you need to put your name and the position number on the bottom of every page, guess what? You put your name and the number on the bottom of every page.

Use a Clean, Professional Font

If the job advertisement does not specify a font and font size then choose a font that is easy on the eye. Good options include:

- Calibri
- Arial
- Garamond
- Verdana
- Times New Roman

Keep the size readable. Usually, 10.5 to 12 point for body text works well, which is slightly smaller than the font on this page.

Avoid decorative fonts, compressed fonts, or anything that looks "creative". Consistency matters, use the same font throughout.

Prioritise Readability Over Density

Trying to fit too much onto the page just makes your application hard to read. Write efficiently and leave space to help the panel members assess your application. You should avoid using a tiny font, narrow margins and having big slabs of text to meet the page restrictions. Instead:

- Use reasonable margins
- Break text into short paragraphs or preferably dot points
- Leave space between sections

White space is not wasted space, it helps the reader process the information in your resume.

Use Bullet Points

When used well bullet points help you:

- Highlight achievements
- Show impact
- Improve readability

Streamlining your application

If you're looking for words to remove this list is a good start as they often don't add any value.

Attempt	Strive
Ensure	Always
Focus on	Required to
I think	Needed to
I could	Able to
I usually	At the end of the day
I might	All things considered

Take this sentence for example,

"I always strive to remain focussed on attempting to ensure that I achieve the required stakeholder engagement outcomes at the end of the day."

It uses a lot of words to say not much, a better sentence is

"I engage with stakeholders through regular meetings, being curious what they are working on, identifying connections between our work and achieving what I agree to. I did this when working in…"

Inside the Interview Room

I have seen panels remove applications from the shortlist because they did not include the candidates name and the position number on the bottom of every page.

The goal is to stay in the process as long as possible so make sure you're doing everything you can to stay there.

Don't write about how you can follow instructions if you are unable to demonstrate that you can.

Reflection: How strong is my example?

Use STAR and STAR+ to write your answer to an interview question.

Are the Situation, Task, Action (use the seesaw) and Result clear?

Have you addressed the Strategic Impact, your Thinking, Applicability of the outlined skills or a Reflection on what you would do differently next time?

Have you removed any filler words that aren't adding value?

How has my answer improved by applying these frameworks?

Chapter Summary

Writing a strong application is about clarity, structure, and evidence. When you use STAR and STAR + thoughtfully, and balance your language with the seesaw, you make it easy for panels to see your capability.

This chapter has shown you how to move from vague claims to concrete examples. It has given you tools to describe your work holistically, confidently, and at the right level. It has also reminded you that details matter, following instructions, streamlining your language, and presenting your application professionally are all part of demonstrating credibility.

When these elements come together, your application stops feeling like guesswork. It becomes a clear, well organised case for why you meet the requirements of the role.

In Chapter 6, we shift focus to your resume. We will explore how to present your career history in a way that complements your application, reinforces your examples, and positions you strongly.

CHAPTER 6:
Writing an APS resume

In this chapter, we focus on building a resume that works with your application, not against it. You will learn how to design a clear, professional document that highlights what matters most about your experience and makes life easy for panel members. We will explore practical choices around layout, structure and language, show you how to turn responsibilities into achievement statements, and look at how to present the full range of your experience with credibility and confidence. Used well, your resume becomes a supporting document that reinforces your story and strengthens everything else you submit.

"Your resume is not a record of
everything you've done.
It is a carefully chosen story about what
matters most for this role."

A good APS resume isn't about telling your whole career story. It's about making it easy for a panel member to understand who you are, what you're good at and how your experience aligns with the role you're applying for.

I want to start by addressing format and then cover what content to include as both are important.

Keep It to Two-ish Pages

As a general rule, aim for two pages, three at the most. Not one page that cuts out important experience and definitely not five pages that no one will read.

Two-ish pages allows you to:

- Show your career progression
- Highlight key achievements
- Provide enough context and information on what you'll bring to the role.

Use Clear Headings and Structure

At minimum, include clear sections such as:

- Name and Contact Details
- Professional Summary (optional)
- Education and Training
- Work Experience
- Other Relevant Experience

Use bold headings, leave white space and separate sections clearly.

Use Bullet Points

For each role, aim for three to five strong bullet points focused on outcomes and achievements *(see Achievement Statements later in this chapter)*.

For your current role use present tense for your Action Verbs, for previous roles use past tense. E.g.

Current	Previous
Leading	Led
Delivering	Delivered
Driving	Drove
Engaging	Engaged

Be Consistent With Formatting

Inconsistency creates distraction, so make sure:

- Dates are formatted the same way
- Job titles follow the same style
- Bullet points align properly
- Capitalisation is consistent

These small details signal professionalism and care and panels will notice.

Make It Easy for the Panel to Read

Panel members are reviewing multiple applications in a short period of time. They are switching between pitches or selection criteria, and later interview notes, referee reports, and resumes as well as trying to get their job done.

A well laid out resume helps the panel quickly understand who you are, what you have done, and how your experience fits the role. A poorly laid out one forces them to work too hard and unfortunately can result in your application being put in the pile of not successful applications.

Contact details

Make your contact details impossible to miss. Your name, phone number and email should be clear and easy to find. It sounds basic, but it's surprisingly common for applicants to bury phone numbers, use outdated email addresses or have headers cluttered with lots of information in their resume. Panels shouldn't have to scroll or search to work out how to contact you.

Use a personal email address over your current work one. Please make sure it is a professional email address not the one you created in high school to impress your friends.

Also, the APSC advise *"there's no need to include your age, gender, or marital status"* so leave them out.

Applicant Tracking Systems (ATS)

Before a person reads your application, there's a good chance a system will. An Applicant Tracking System, or ATS, is used by many organisations to manage recruitment. They store applications, help panels review candidates, and in some cases filter or rank applications based on how well they match the role.

You don't know what system is being used by the organisation you're applying to so your application needs to be clear, readable, and aligned to the role, not just for a human reader, but for the system as well.

How ATS works (in practice)

An ATS doesn't "understand" your experience in the way a person does, it scans and parses your resume and application to identify:

- keywords that match the job description
- job titles and dates
- skills, capabilities, and qualifications
- structure and formatting

If your resume is overly complex, heavily designed, or missing key language from the job ad, the system may not interpret it correctly and that can mean a human never looks at your resume because some systems automatically reject applications if it can't find the relevant information.

Common mistakes to avoid

Some of the most common issues I see include:

- Using overly designed resumes with columns, graphics, or text boxes
- Uploading scanned PDFs that can't be read properly by the system
- Using different language to the job ad
- Burying key information in long paragraphs
- Inconsistent job titles or unclear dates

Note: These things don't just frustrate systems, they frustrate people too.

How to make your resume ATS-friendly

If you do what we've already discussed by using a clean, simple format, stick to a standard structure with clear headings and avoid tables, columns, text boxes, and images your resume will be easier for ATS systems to process.

Use the language of the role

Pay close attention to the wording in the job ad. If the role is asking for "stakeholder engagement" or "policy development," use those exact terms where they genuinely reflect your experience.

Be clear and specific

List your roles, organisations, and dates clearly. Use bullet points to highlight responsibilities and achievements as this makes it easy for humans and machines to scan.

Focus on substance over style

A visually impressive resume won't help if the content isn't clear, prioritise clarity, relevance, and alignment.

Choose the right file format

When in doubt, use a Word document or a simple PDF (not scanned) and make sure the text can be selected and copied.

Align to the criteria

Even if the system isn't filtering heavily, the panel will be. Make sure your resume and supporting statements clearly reflect the capabilities being assessed.

Now we've got the structure laid out properly, let's discuss what content needs to go where to support your application.

Put Your Most Recent Role First

Always list your experience in reverse chronological order. That means start with your most recent role, then work backwards.

Panels want to see:

- What you are doing now
- Your current level of responsibility
- How you have progressed

Do not make them hunt for this information, for each role, clearly include:

- Job title
- Organisation with a brief description
- Dates (month and year) you started and finished
- Brief description of the role and your achievements

Make Key Information Easy to Find

Ask yourself, can someone reading my resume quickly find:

- My current role?
- My level?

- My main responsibilities?
- My strongest achievements?
- My contact details?

If not, update your resume so that they can, as resumes are often used as reference documents during interviews. Panel members glance at them to refresh their memory or clarify details so if yours is easy to navigate, it will work in your favour.

Telling Your Story Well

Put the most relevant information for the job you're applying for at the top throughout. Panels should not have to hunt for the skills, knowledge and experience that matter most for this role.

If the job ad emphasises stakeholder engagement, project delivery and executive briefing, those capabilities should be mirrored in the order you describe your strengths and achievements in each role you list. You should have the stakeholder engagement first, then your project delivery and finally brief writing skills. This helps the reader subconsciously connect the dots and further reduces their cognitive load.

If role titles are obscure or it is unclear what you did, include a quick note to explain it can be helpful. If you've held multiple roles in a short period, stepped back a level, changed fields or taken a career break, include a brief explanation, one line is often enough.

Panels notice patterns, and silence invites assumptions. A simple, neutral explanation helps the reader stay focused on your capability rather than speculating about your history.

Be selective about what you include don't treat your resume as a career archive. If you received a Staff Member of the Month award twenty years ago, I get it, you are proud and you be. But it doesn't help assess your current capability. Focus on recent, relevant achievements that show how you work now. If something doesn't strengthen your case for this role, it probably doesn't belong.

> **Tip:** I have a version of my resume that has my whole career captured in it. From my first role stacking shelves at a major supermarket chain to what I do now as a leadership development consultant and executive coach. This version of my resume sits on my computer and will never be sent out. It's there for me to have a career history for myself to look back on.
>
> When it's time to share my resume I save a new version of the document and include only the relevant information for the role I'm applying for to keep it to 2-3 pages long.

Getting the format and structure of your resume right is like setting the frame for a good picture. It makes your application easy to read, easy to follow, and easy to take seriously. But structure alone is never enough. Once the layout is doing its job, the real work begins. What matters most is what you place inside that frame. This is where achievement statements come in. They move your resume from being a tidy list of roles and duties to a clear account of the value you have created, the problems you have solved, and the impact you have had.

Achievement Statements

Achievement statements are one of the easiest ways to strengthen your resume. Most APS applicants list responsibilities, which tell the panel what you were *expected* to do. Achievements, on the other hand, show what you *actually* delivered. They highlight your impact, not just your duties, and they help you stand out in a pool of very similar applicants.

A responsibility sounds like this:

Managed the team inbox.

It's functional, but it doesn't show capability. Writing this as an achievement turns the same work into evidence of your skills and ability:

Improved inbox management by introducing a triage system that reduced response times from five days to two.

Same task, very different impression and a better demonstration of what you actually did to "manage the team inbox".

A helpful way to write strong achievement statements is to think in three parts:

Action + Outcome + Evidence.

Action is the verb or what you did, reference the ILS to make sure you are accurately capturing the level of your work.

Outcome is the improvement or benefit. What changed.

Evidence is any data you can use to back it up.

This might be numbers, feedback, time saved or even a qualitative shift like reduced frustration from staff.

Here's an example to illustrate the difference.

Responsibility:

Prepared monthly reports.

Achievement:

Streamlined the monthly reporting process by removing duplicate data requests, which cut preparation time by four hours and improved accuracy.

Again, same task but a far clearer picture of capability.

If you feel stuck, start by listing your responsibilities as they are. Then ask yourself:

- What did I improve?
- What did I create?
- What did I fix?
- What did I deliver faster, more accurately or more efficiently?
- What feedback did I receive that reflects impact?
- What changed because I was there?

Even small changes count, you don't need dramatic results for achievements to matter. Panels simply want to see evidence of contribution and competence.

For example, if your responsibility was *supporting a project team*, your achievements might include:

Coordinating version control for project documents to reduce errors and rework.

or

Building relationships with three key stakeholders to increase cooperation and speed up approvals.

Both are modest but meaningful and tell the panel you aren't just present, you are contributing.

When you rewrite responsibilities as achievements, your resume immediately feels stronger, clearer and more credible.

Plus you're giving the panel exactly what they need to assess you by providing behavioural evidence and you're setting yourself up for stronger selection criteria and interview examples, because your resume now speaks the same language as the rest of the documentation you submit as part of the recruitment process.

Exercise: Rewrite responsibilities as achievements

Take a few minutes and rewrite Responsibilities as Achievements using the structure:

Action + Outcome + Evidence.

Including Experience Outside of Paid Work

Some of the most important skills you bring to work were built doing things away from the office.

Your resume does not have to be limited to formal, paid employment. In fact, some of the most relevant experience you bring may come from things you have done outside of work.

This might include:

- Volunteering roles
- Board or committee membership
- Community or sporting club leadership
- Podcasting, blogging or professional contributions
- Study combined with part time work
- Periods of parenting or caring

What matters to panels is not where the experience came from, but that it demonstrates the skills, behaviours and capability required for the role you are applying for.

When including experience outside of paid work, use the same principles you would for any role:

- Focus on skills and behaviours, not just activities
- Highlight leadership, collaboration, problem solving and organisation where you've done them
- Where possible, show outcomes or impact by including achievements not just responsibilities

This approach is especially helpful if:

- You are changing careers
- You are returning to the workforce
- You have taken time out for caring responsibilities
- You are early in your career and building your experience base

Your resume is a story about your capability and readiness for the role you are applying for not just a list of jobs. Make sure it tells your story clearly, honestly and in a way that reflects the full range of experience you bring.

Inside the Interview Room

I once sat on a panel where a dad was returning to work after spending time at home raising his young children, who were about to start school.

Instead of leaving a gap on his resume, he listed this period as a role and described the responsibilities through a capability lens. He talked about managing complex stakeholder needs, coordinating schedules and logistics, negotiating priorities, and maintaining communication across multiple moving parts.

It landed extremely well with the panel. It showed maturity, self awareness and transferable skill, and it meant there was no awkward question about a "gap" in his work history. It was simply another chapter in his professional story.

Reflection: What strengths do I want to share

What strengths do you want the panel to see clearly in the first half page of your resume?

How do they align with the job requirements?

Using AI to Support Your Resume

I appreciate that resumes take time to write, update, and tailor for each job and that they are often prepared under pressure of deadlines and completed in personal time.

AI can help you present your experience clearly and strategically. If it is used poorly, it can make your resume generic, exaggerated, or misleading.

Remember: Your resume must remain your story, told accurately and credibly, don't just copy what AI provides into your application and submit it.

Start With Your Real Career Story

Before using AI, clarify your own history, build a list that covers your:

- Roles and responsibilities
- Major achievements
- Development milestones
- Transitions and changes

If you skip this step, you risk losing accuracy and nuance. AI should refine your story, not invent it.

Strengthening Achievement Statements

AI is particularly useful for improving achievement statements.

You might ask:

"Make this more outcome focused."

"Strengthen this with evidence."

or

"Turn this into a clear achievement."

This helps shift from task descriptions to impact statements.

Tailoring to Specific Roles

AI can support targeted applications. For example:

"Compare my resume with this job ad."

"Where should I emphasise alignment?"

or

"What gaps do I need to address?"

This reduces the risk of sending generic resumes and supports strategic positioning of your skills.

Checking Level and Language

You can use AI to assess whether your language matches the role. You might ask:

"Is this pitched at the right level for an EL1 application?"

"Where am I underselling myself?"

or

"Where am I overstating impact?"

Accurate pitching protects credibility and opportunity.

Supporting Career Transitions

AI can help you frame:

- Sector changes
- Career breaks
- Part time work
- Returns from leave
- Diverse role histories

You might ask:

"Highlight transferable skills from my resume for this role."

or

"Help me frame this transition positively."

A Practical Workflow

1. Draft your resume manually

2. Refine responsibilities into achievements

3. Align your skills to the role

4. Check level and language are appropriate

5. Personalise the tone so it's your work

6. Do a final manual review to confirm

Before submitting, ask:

"Could I confidently explain every line in an interview?"

If not, go back and rewrite it using your words so that you can.

Applicant Tracking Systems (ATS) Compatibility

You can also use AI tools to check how your resume will perform in an ATS. Paste your resume alongside the job ad and ask the tool to simulate how an ATS might interpret your document or suggest a more ATS-friendly structure. Again, the key is not to blindly accept the output, but to use it as a second set of eyes.

Example Resumes

Over the following pages are two resumes from the same fictional candidate, with the same roles, tenure, and career progression. On paper, both look solid and both would likely pass an initial scan.

However, only one gives a panel what they need to confidently assess performance at the EL2 level. The difference is not the experience, it's how that experience is translated into evidence.

As you read, notice what each version emphasises, what it leaves out, and how easy it is to understand the candidate's actual impact. They're formatted the same way to make it easy to compare them.

Example Resume 1 – A stronger resume

Jordan Taylor | jordan.taylor@email.com | 0400 000 000

Profile

Demonstrated track record of leading complex policy and program initiatives across government agencies at the EL2 level. Known for shaping strategy, influencing stakeholders, and delivering outcomes in ambiguous environments in the Improved Social Outcomes Policy Package Program.

Education

Bachelor of Public Policy and Management

University of Canberra

Professional Development

APS Leadership Advantage Program

Coaching for Performance (internal program)

Professional Experience

Acting EL2, Strategic Policy and Reform

Department of Social Outcomes   Jan 2025 – Present (Acting)

Led a multidisciplinary team of 12 to deliver a high-profile policy package within tight timeframes, achieving on-time submission with positive Ministerial feedback

Influenced senior stakeholders to resolve competing priorities, evidenced by agreement on a unified implementation roadmap and reduced delivery risk

EL1, Policy and Program Delivery

Department of Social Outcomes   Jul 2023 – Jan 2025

Led the design and implementation of a national pilot program, reaching over 3,000 participants, exceeding participation targets by 25%

Delivered complex briefing and advice to SES and Ministers, contributing to 10+ key decisions with no rework required

Strengthened program governance by introducing new reporting frameworks, reducing reporting errors by 40%

EL1, Stakeholder Engagement and Partnerships

Department of Community Wellbeing   Jan 2022 – Jun 2023

Built strategic partnerships with state and territory counterparts, resulting in co-designed initiatives adopted across 4 jurisdictions

Navigated sensitive stakeholder environments, resolving long-standing issues and securing agreement on shared policy positions

Embedded a structured engagement approach, increasing stakeholder satisfaction scores from 68% to 87%

APS6, Policy Officer

Department of Community Wellbeing   Jul 2020 – Dec 2021

Developed policy proposals informed by data and consultation, contributing to successful Budget measures totalling $20M

Coordinated cross-agency input for major submissions, ensuring consistency and quality under tight deadlines

Resume Example 2: A weaker resume

Jordan Taylor

Profile

Experienced policy professional with a strong background in government. Skilled in stakeholder engagement, program delivery, and policy development. Proven ability to work in fast-paced environments and manage competing priorities.

Education

Bachelor of Public Policy and Management

University of Canberra

Professional Development

Various internal training courses

Workshops and seminars

Professional Experience

Acting EL2, Strategic Policy and Reform

Department of Social Outcomes   Jan 2025 – Present (Acting)

Responsible for leading policy reform work across multiple areas

Managed a team to support delivery of key priorities

Provided advice to senior executives and contributed to decision-making processes

EL1, Policy and Program Delivery

Department of Social Outcomes   Jul 2023 – Jan 2025

Led policy and program work in line with government priorities

Prepared briefs and submissions for senior stakeholders

Oversaw implementation of program activities and reporting requirements

EL1, Stakeholder Engagement and Partnerships

Department of Community Wellbeing   Jan 2022 – Jun 2023

Engaged with internal and external stakeholders on policy matters

Supported collaboration across jurisdictions

Contributed to stakeholder engagement strategies and activities

APS6, Policy Officer

Department of Community Wellbeing   Jul 2020 – Dec 2021

Assisted with development of policy proposals

Coordinated input for briefs and submissions

Undertook research and analysis to inform decision-making

Panels are assessing judgement, impact, and readiness for the next level and the stronger resume makes this easier for them. It outlines clear actions, links them to outcomes, and backs it up with evidence through scale, influence, and leadership consistent with EL2 expectations.

The weaker version, while credible, forces the panel to guess. It lists responsibilities, uses safe language, and lacks proof of effectiveness. In feedback, this candidate would likely hear phrases like "we couldn't fully assess your impact," "unclear on the scale of work," or "not enough evidence of operating at level." The difference lies in articulating what you've already done in a way that demonstrates your value.

Reality check

We've probably spent more time on this chapter than the panel will spend reading your resume. In most APS processes, resumes are used to refresh memory, confirm timelines or answer specific questions. The heavy lifting happens in your selection criteria and interview. That's not a reason to underinvest in your resume. It's a reason to make it clear, relevant and easy to scan.

Chapter Summary

A strong APS resume is about making your capability easy to see. When your layout is clean, achievements are clear, and language is aligned to the role, you remove unnecessary barriers between your experience and the panel understanding.

This chapter has shown you how to move from listing duties to demonstrating impact. It has encouraged you to be selective, honest, and thoughtful about how you present yourself. It has also reinforced that experience comes in many forms, and that well framed non traditional pathways can be powerful evidence of capability.

Used alongside your application and interview examples, your resume becomes part of a coherent narrative. It supports your claims, reinforces your level, and helps panels trust what they are reading.

In Chapter 7, we shift from documents to you. We focus on how to prepare mentally and physically for interviews, manage nerves, build confidence, and perform at your best on the day. Because strong preparation is not just about what you say, it is about how you show up.

CHAPTER 7:
Preparing for your interview

In this chapter, we focus on how to prepare in a way that builds confidence and reduces pressure. You will learn how to consolidate your examples, practise effectively, and create routines that help you stay calm and focused in the days and hours leading up to your interview.

We will look at practical strategies for in person, virtual, and pre recorded interviews, and explore how to use AI tools as part of your preparation without becoming dependent on them.

"Clarity creates calm.
Calm creates credibility."

Preparation is less about trying to be perfect and more about creating the conditions for you to perform at your best.

My recommended approach is not to memorise answers or rehearse until you sound scripted. It's to create enough familiarity that you can think clearly, respond thoughtfully and stay present under pressure. When you prepare well, you walk into the interview calmer, more grounded and better able to show who you really are.

One Week Out

Start by rereading the job description (this is why I recommended you save a copy) and your application as if you're seeing it for the first time. These are the claims you've already made about yourself, and the panel will be testing them. Make sure you can comfortably talk to every example you have included.

Identify a small bank of strong examples that cover common interview themes such as stakeholder engagement, prioritisation, dealing with ambiguity, collaboration and judgement. Many examples can be adapted across questions so you don't need dozens, you just need a few that are relevant and that you deeply understand.

Practise STAR examples each day, out loud. Out loud matters more than you think, speaking your examples helps you find your natural pacing, notice where you over explain and identify where you need to tighten things. Remember, you're not trying to memorise scripts, you're building familiarity and fluency with your experience and the structure.

Revisit the ILS behaviours at the level you're applying for. Ask yourself where your examples show autonomy, influence and complexity that match that level. This is often the difference between a good answer and a strong one.

> **Inside the interview room**
>
> Someone I worked with through interview preparation coaching used the STAR framework with her partner when they got home from work and were asked "how was your day?" While clunky at first, it got better every day as she got more used to the framework. Thankfully, she gave her partner a warning that she intended to start responding that way so it wasn't super weird for him.

Ask for feedback from a colleague, coach or trusted peer. Even one practice question with honest feedback can surface blind spots and build confidence.

You might use a phone or computer to record yourself answering questions and then watch them back. While this can be uncomfortable you will pickup communication habits that you were unaware you had by doing this.

When I started my podcast I was unaware how often I started a sentence with "So…" or "Now…" until I listened to a few episodes. It still happens every now and then but mostly I'm on top of it. This is important to be aware of because the habit diminishes the point I am making. As do excessive "ums", "ahs", "you knows", "likes", and "oks".

The Night Before

The night before is not the time for cramming. At this point, your preparation shifts from learning to settling.

Reread your application once, slowly for the final time. Remind yourself of the examples you've chosen and the strengths you want to convey, then put it all away so you don't feel pressure to remember everything.

Prepare your clothes for the interview so that one less decision sits in your head on interview day. Choose something comfortable and professional that allows you to focus on the conversation rather than how you feel. I suggest that you +1 your outfit from what it normally is. Just take it up one notch and at a minimum make sure your shoes are clean.

I also recommend to people that they have a second outfit with them on interview day. I've seen people show up for interviews with a coffee stain on their shirt and while it didn't impact the panel's opinion it obviously distracted them and impacted their performance.

Make space to relax, go for a walk, eat something nourishing, and try to get a decent night's sleep.

One Hour Before

The final hour is about regulation, not reviewing your application and examples. Whether your interview is face to face or virtual spend it doing something that helps you feel calm and centred. That might be breathing, stretching, listening to music, walking or sitting quietly. Book this time out in your calendar and let your manager know you'll be away from your desk, take leave if you have to. You don't want to be caught in a meeting that's running long when you should be on your way to your interview.

> **Tip:** If your interview is face to face get to the location before you start these activities. Arrive with enough time to find a carpark and get settled.

Please don't arrive at the building too early as panels are often interviewing other candidates and may not be available. Turning up too early can come across as inconsiderate which can have a negative impact. It can also undo all your good regulation work if you are waiting in the foyer for a long time for someone to come and meet you.

Preparing for a Virtual Interview

Virtual interviews are more common across much of the APS, and a small amount of preparation here can make a big difference to how you're perceived. The aim is to reduce or remove distractions so the panel can focus on you.

Preparing your device

Have the device fully charged and plugged in, make sure any updates have been completed they day before the interview time and that you've recently restarted it so it will stay on for your whole interview.

Lighting

Ideally, have light coming from in front of you so your face is clearly lit. Natural light works well if it's available but you can setup a lamp if you need to. Try to avoid strong backlighting by having uncovered windows or lamps behind you, as this can leave you in shadow and make it harder for the panel to read your facial expressions. You don't want to look like you're in witness protection.

Camera setup

Get your camera up to eye level and avoid using a laptop or tablet camera sitting on a desk. The first time you look up to think about an answer, the panel will see straight up your nose, which isn't anyone's best angle. A stand, a stack of books or an external webcam can easily fix this and help you appear more present and engaged.

Where to look

Try to position the panel's videos on your screen as close to your camera as possible so that when you're speaking, it appears as though you're making eye contact. Avoid placing the panel's video off to the side as it can look like you're looking away or are distracted which is confusing.

Logging in

Have the interview link ready to go well before the scheduled time. Close unnecessary tabs, silence notifications and log in 5-10 minutes early so you're not flustered at the start.

If you can, have a backup internet option such as a mobile hotspot ready, just in case.

Notes

Some people find it useful to have notes with them for their interview. They distract me so I don't use them but if they work for you, just use them. Don't have them on post it notes stuck around the edge of the monitor or on the wall behind it. It looks and sounds like you're reading the answers even if you think it doesn't. Have them organised and easily accessible on a note pad near you. You may even want to flag with the panel that you have them so they don't have to guess what you are doing when you look away from the camera to read them.

Noise

Minimise noise in the environment you are in. If you're at work, book a meeting room out for 15-30 minutes before and after the interview and get away from your desk. If you're at home, try and have the house to yourself or be in an area you can keep as quiet as possible.

What if I can't

I acknowledge that there is an element of privilege in all of this. I'm lucky to have fast internet, a good webcam and microphone, a quiet space and decent lighting, I acknowledge not everyone does or can. If you can't achieve these conditions, let the panel know early. A simple explanation at the start is enough, then let it go and don't keep apologising. Panels are generally understanding, and your capability is not defined by your technology.

Pre Recorded Interviews: When the Screen Is the Panel

Increasingly, APS recruitment processes include pre recorded interviews. Instead of sitting in front of a live panel, you are given access to an online platform that presents questions one at a time and records your responses for later review.

Typically, you will see a question on screen, be given a short period to think, and then a set amount of time to record your answer. Once you start recording, you cannot pause, restart, or redo it. What you say is what the panel will see.

This format can feel strange and impersonal, but the assessment principles are exactly the same. Panel members will still be listening for evidence, structure, clarity, and alignment with the role and the ILS behaviours. They are simply doing it later, on screen, rather than live.

Preparation is similar you need to practise answering questions out loud, get comfortable speaking to a camera and time yourself so you know what your natural answer length is.

Again, you need to make sure your space is quiet, your lighting is good, and your camera is positioned well.

Most importantly, bring the same energy and professionalism you would to a live interview. Sit up, make eye contact with the camera, speak clearly, and treat each answer as if real people are sitting in front of you. Because they will be, just not in real time.

Think of pre recorded interviews as playing an away game without a crowd. It feels different, but the rules have not changed.

Using AI to Prepare for an Interview

AI can help you prepare more strategically for interviews. You can upload a job ad and ask it to generate likely questions based on capabilities, responsibilities, and technical requirements.

From there, you can draft STAR or STAR+ responses in your own words and ask:

- "Does this demonstrate the required behaviours?"
- "Where is the evidence weak?"
- "Is this appropriate for this level?"

Used this way, AI highlights gaps rather than writing scripts for you.

Stress Testing Your Examples

You can ask AI to act as a panel member and assess your responses. For example:

- "Does this show APS6 decision making?"
- "Does this demonstrate sufficient autonomy?"
- "Where could this be stronger?"

Like every other tool in this book, the value of AI output depends on how deliberately you use it.

Reflection: What helps me best prepare?

What helps me to feel calm and confident?

Thinking about your best interview how did you prepare beforehand?

Chapter Summary

Strong interview preparation is about building familiarity, confidence, and trust that you can think clearly under pressure.

When you know your examples, and have practised out loud, you reduce uncertainty and increase your ability to stay present.

This chapter has shown you how to prepare by reviewing and refining your examples, managing your energy, and setting yourself up well for different types of interviews, each step supports your performance rather than feeling overwhelmed.

In Chapter 8, we turn our attention to what happens once the interview begins. We will explore how to manage nerves in the room, build rapport with panels, structure your answers in real time, and recover when things do not go exactly to plan.

CHAPTER 8:
During the interview

In this chapter, we focus on how to approach interviews with confidence, clarity, and perspective. You will learn how to reframe the concerns people have about interviews, structure strong answers, handle both common and unexpected questions, and stay grounded when things feel challenging.

We will explore practical frameworks such as The Funnel, STAR and STAR +, look at ways to avoid over scripting, and strategies for getting unstuck.

"An interview is a conversation about whether you, this role and this team belong together."

The aim is not to perform a flawless interview, but to show up as a capable, thoughtful professional who can communicate their value clearly and calmly.

Interview principles to focus on

I like to focus on these principles for every interview I go to, they help me approach them feeling more calm and confident:

- The panel want you to do well
- You're a world leading expert on you
- You're assessing the panel too
- You're already in elite company by getting to interview
- You can't control the outcome

The panel want you to do well.

The panel have selected you from a list of potentially hundreds of other applicants to attend an interview. They are demonstrating their belief that there is value in interviewing you and having you provide further information on your skills, qualifications, experience and value you would bring to the role they are advertising.

You are being interviewed on something you're a world leading expert in

There is no one in the world that knows more about you than you. All you need to do is get that expertise out of your head and into the recruitment process. Moving from guesswork to framework, preparing and practicing are going to increase the likelihood of you doing this.

You are interviewing the panel as much as they are interviewing you.

You are also deciding whether this organisation, team and role are the right ones for you. You could be offered the job at the end of the process and not accept it. While this is unlikely, I have seen it happen and awareness of this can help to reduce the power imbalance some people feel during the process.

You're already in elite company

By the interview stage you're already in the top 5-10% of candidates who applied, congratulations and well done.

If you were top 5 to 10 % in anything else in the world you would be very excited.

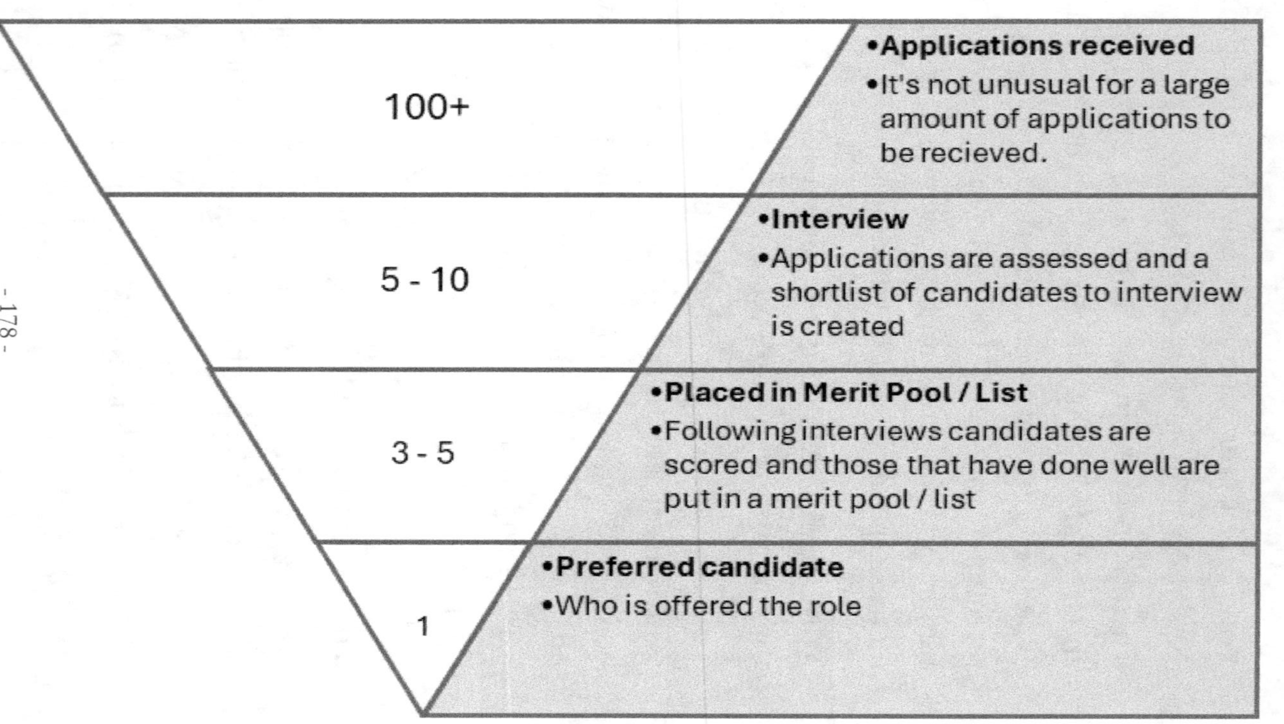
100+
•Applications received
•It's not unusual for a large amount of applications to be recieved.
5 - 10
•Interview
•Applications are assessed and a shortlist of candidates to interview is created
3 - 5
•Placed in Merit Pool / List
•Following interviews candidates are scored and those that have done well are put in a merit pool / list
1
•Preferred candidate
•Who is offered the role

Also, if you saw the number of applicants and thought that's a lot, it's a conservative number. I've heard from panel chairs that they regularly get well over that number, sometimes 500+ but the numbers are easier to work out with 100.

You can't control the outcome so don't worry about it

You can't make the panel select you, all you can do is influence them by demonstrating you're the best candidate for the role they are advertising.

In the recruitment process you also can't control:

- Who else applies,
- How other people perform in the process,
- What the panel are looking for,

What you can control and therefore should invest your time in is:

- How you prepare for your interview,
- Whether you practice and get feedback or not,
- Doing things that will help you present your best case for why they should hire you in your interview.

Tip: One of the best ways to get better at recruitment is to sit on a recruitment panel. If you are working in the public service include it in your development goals at your next performance discussion and look for opportunities.

If you haven't been on a recruitment panel yet work hard to make that happen, you'll learn things that will improve your performance.

As a panel member you not only get to read and hear lots of responses to questions you also get access to the panel discussion afterwards which helps inform you on what panels are looking for.

Now let's look at some common questions that are asked at interviews and how you might go about being more prepared to answer them.

The "What attracted you to the role?" question

This is a common question to start interviews, and in my experience it is often not answered well. Sometimes this question is just an ice breaker, sometimes it is a scored question. Either way ultimately you want to start strong and make the panel feel comfortable that they have made the right choice in inviting you to an interview.

People have responded with "I want a promotion", "I want more money" or "I don't like my current job". While they may be true, they are not great and a missed opportunity.

My assumption is that you are a highly capable, well educated, intelligent human being and you could choose to work anywhere. Use this answer to explain why you want to work for this organisation, in this team, at this level, in this role.

To do this you can use a structure which I call "The Funnel" as it starts wide and gets narrow.

The Funnel

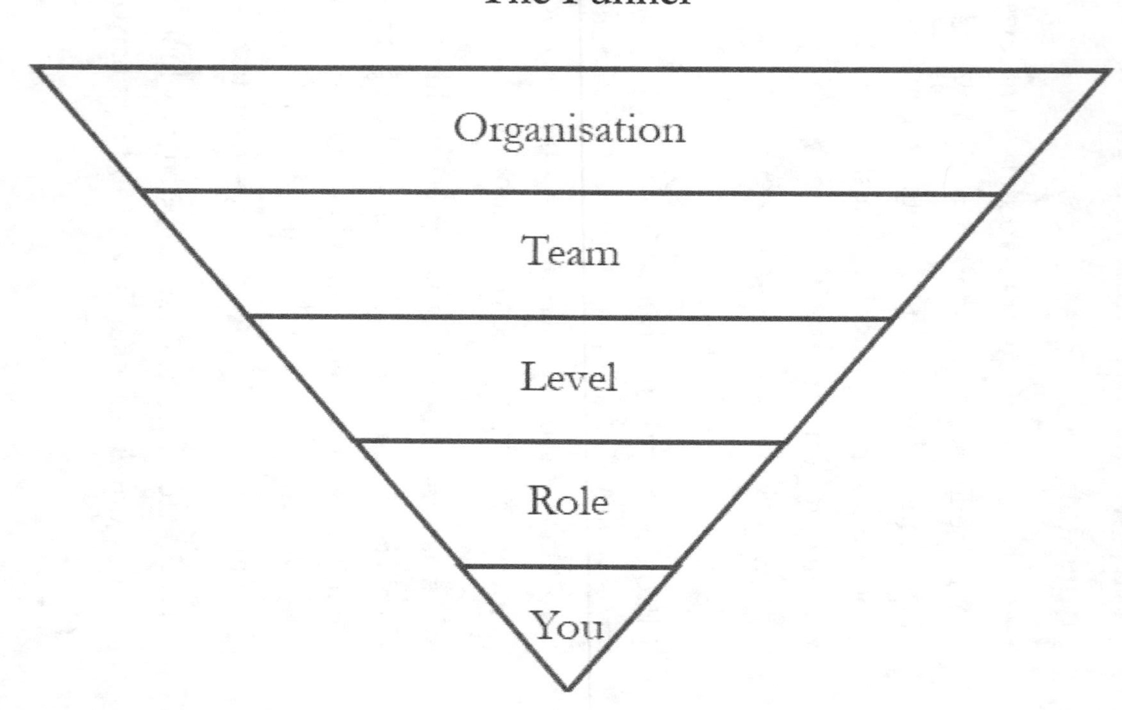

Use the following questions and prompts to plan
and practice your answer.

Organisation	What excites you about working for this organisation? What strategic objectives would you like to help achieve? Why is the organisation's vision and mission something you're passionate about?
Team	What excites you about this team? What do you hope to learn from working in the team?
Level	In a bulk round the role this is unlikely to be specifically defined. In that case what about the level and what interests you.
Role	What is your understanding of the role? What do you hope to achieve in the role?
You	What will you bring to the role? Keep it short as you don't want to give too many examples away that you'll use later.

You don't have to get it "perfect" every time but you want to make sure you can easily talk to most of these key points.

People often ask "can I use it the other way and start with me and move to organisation?" Absolutely, do whatever feels most natural and comfortable for you. An organisation first approach works best for me, so I start there.

By structuring your answer using this model you can make sure you touch on all the things that you know about the organisation and role and what you would bring to them. The added benefit with this structure is if you get lost in your answer, as I've experienced during interviews, you can just move to the next part of the model.

For example, if you have started sharing your answer and you have spent a lot of time talking about the level and why that level is attractive to you, what you think you could bring to the level and what you see is the responsibilities of the level. You notice that you're rambling. What I've seen many people do is keep talking in the hope that their brain will catch up and their brain doesn't catch up and so they don't get back on topic and they ramble and ramble. The panel notice it and the applicant notices it and they feel more and more uncomfortable and nervous and therefore can't think of what they should be saying and get more and more lost in their answer.

I've intentionally tried to capture some of this in the way I've written the previous paragraph.

If you notice this happening and you have this structure in your head, you can just move to the next thing. I'm rambling oh next I'm talking about the role and what I would bring to it. The next words out of your mouth are "and what I would bring to the role is…" and the rest of your answer will flow from there and you'll be back on track.

Inside the Interview Room

I was a part of bulk round recruitment for a government agency that was comprised of multiple people being interviewed across multiple days. How much people had prepared was obvious as the answers were given so close together.

When asked why they applied for the job answers ranged from:

"I'm not really sure why I applied."

"I just applied for every available position at this level."

"I'm excited to potentially join the *organisation* to contribute to achieving *organisations' purpose statement*. I've been studying *area of role responsibility* where I specialised in *relevant sub area* and achieved high marks. In my current part time role I have developed skills relevant to the job role and would apply these if selected for the role."

By preparing, thinking about answers to potential questions and showing up calm, confident and relaxed the last applicant far out performed the others.

The "tell us a bit about yourself" question.

Another common interview question, that is misunderstood and often poorly answered. It is not an invitation to walk through your life story or recite your full CV. Your answer shapes how the panel sees you from the very beginning of the interview and allows you to position yourself as someone who will strengthen their team.

It is as an opportunity to explain why you are a good fit for this role, team and organisation.

Keep It Role-Focused, Not Biography-Focused

One of the biggest mistakes people make is treating this question like a personal introduction:

"I grew up in regional NSW, studied commerce, then worked in three different departments..."

This may be interesting, but it is rarely useful to the panel. Instead, filter your story through the lens of, "What parts of my background best explain why I will do well in this role?"

If something does not help answer that question, it probably does not belong in your response.

What the Panel Is Really Listening For

When interviewers ask this question, they are quietly assessing three things:

- What are your core strengths?
- How do you see yourself professionally?
- How will you add value to this team and workplace?

They want to understand not just what you have done, but who you are at work and how that shows up in your everyday behaviour.

How to Structure Your Answer

A strong response usually has three parts:

- Your professional identity
- Your key strengths and experience
- Your contribution to their team

Let's deep dive each of them with some examples.

Your Professional Identity

Start with how you see yourself in your work. This might include your main area of expertise, your approach, or what you are known for.

For example:

"I'm a policy professional who enjoys working at the intersection of evidence, stakeholder engagement, and practical delivery."

Your Key Strengths and Experience

Briefly highlight two or three strengths that are directly relevant to the role. Use concrete language and, where possible, link them to actual experience.

For example:

"Over the past five years, I've built strong skills in project coordination, briefing senior leaders, and working across complex teams. This is best demonstrated through my work with..."

Ways to show How You Strengthen the Team

Strong answers go beyond individual achievement, they show how you make others better.

You might reference:

- How you support colleagues
- How you contribute to culture
- How you handle pressure
- How you build trust
- How you share knowledge

For example:

"I'm known for being someone people can rely on, especially during busy periods. I focus on clear communication and making sure everyone understands priorities."

This signals that you are not just capable, but also constructive to work with.

Your Contribution to Their Team

Finish by connecting who you are to what they need. Aim to show how your strengths will help them perform better as a group.

For example:

"I bring a calm, organised approach and a strong focus on collaboration, which helps teams stay focused and deliver under pressure."

The "What are your strengths?" and "What are your weaknesses?" questions

These two questions show up in many recruitment processes and they sound simple, but they're often where people either undersell themselves or drift into rehearsed, forgettable answers so let's make them useful.

Strengths: you're probably better than you think

One of the biggest challenges with strengths is that the things you're genuinely good at often feel normal to you. They don't feel like strengths because they are *"just how I do things."*

---

*It's hard to see what's on the
label from inside our jar*

That's why generic answers like *"I'm a good communicator"* or *"I work hard"* don't land, they're too abstract and don't help the panel understand what you actually do.

A more effective way to identify your strengths is to start with a real example. Think of an achievement you're proud of, it could be from work, study, volunteering, sport, or life more broadly. Anything that mattered to you and had a positive outcome is a good place to start.

Now, instead of trying to name your strengths straight away, tell that story to someone you trust. Then ask them, *"What strengths did you hear in that story?"*

I've run this activity with lots of groups and the response to that question is often surprising for the story teller.

They might say things like:

- "You brought people together"

- "You stayed calm when things got messy"

- "You made something complicated simple"

- "You backed yourself when it mattered"

Those are your strengths, described in a way that is grounded in real behaviour. Now in an interview, you can then bring those strengths to life by linking them to examples.

"One of my strengths is bringing structure to complex situations. For example…"

This approach helps you speak with more confidence because it's based on something real, and it makes it easier for the panel to see you in the role.

Here's a table of strengths you or the person listening to your story can refer to if needed as often our vocabulary for strengths is lacking.

Accepts others	Flexible	Patient
Analytical	Focussed	Persistent
Appreciate	Forgiving	Playful
Assertive	Friendly	Positive
Athletic	Generous	Problem solver
Brave	Hardworking	Resilient
Caring	Honest	Respectful
Compassionate	Humble	Responsible
Confident	Humour	Self starter
Cooperative	Independent	Share
Creative	Kind	Sociable
Dependable	Loyal	Talented at __
Determined	Motivated	Thoughtful
Empathetic	Open Minded	Trustworthy
Enthusiastic	Optimistic	Understanding

Weaknesses: keep it real, and show how you manage it

Saying you're "a perfectionist", "too committed", or that you "care too much" isn't answering the question. Most panels have heard those answers many times before, and it doesn't tell them anything useful about how you operate.

A stronger approach is to choose a genuine weakness, something that could get in your way if left unmanaged. Then, just as importantly, explain what you do about it.

Panels don't expect candidates to be perfect and to not have any weaknesses, what they are assessing is your level of self-awareness and your ability to manage yourself in the role.

For example, when I'm asked this question, I say:

"One of my weaknesses is that I can become unorganised when I'm under pressure. To manage it, I spend time at the start of each week planning out what needs to get done. I block time in my calendar for the bigger pieces of work, make sure meetings are confirmed, and check I've allowed time for things like travel or preparation. I also build in

time for things that keep me at my best, like getting to the gym."

There are a few things happening in that response:

- The weakness is real and relatable
- It's specific, not vague
- There's a clear strategy to manage it
- It shows ownership and discipline

That's what panels are looking for.

Now that our interview is off to a good start the panel will likely move to behavioural based questions to understand your experience in different areas. First let's look at some common questions and then how to answer them using the STAR and STAR+ frameworks.

Common Interview Questions

While every APS interview is different, most follow a very similar pattern as panels are usually guided by the Integrated Leadership System (ILS) and the levels capability expectations. This means that, regardless of the agency or role, you will often be asked questions that test the same core areas.

Once you understand this, interviews become far more predictable. You are no longer preparing for "random" questions, and you can focus your preparation on known capability themes.

Most APS interviews will include questions about:

- Strategic thinking and direction
- Achieves Results
- Productive Working Relationships
- Drive, Integrity and Professionalism
- Communicates with influence
- Technical capability

Some examples of each are on the following pages. Remember: use action verbs in your answer aligned with the ILS for the level you're applying for.

Strategic Thinking and Direction

These questions test how you think beyond the immediate task and connect your work to bigger priorities.

Examples include:

- "Tell us about a time you had to think strategically."
- "How have you aligned your work with organisational priorities?"
- "Describe a time you had to balance short term pressures with long term goals."
- "How do you consider risk and opportunity in your work?"

What panels are listening for:

- Awareness of broader context
- Understanding of organisational goals
- Ability to think beyond your own role
- Sound decision making

Preparation tip: Choose examples where you had to consider more than just your immediate work.

Achieves Results

These questions focus on delivery. They test whether you can turn plans into outcomes.

Examples include:

- "Tell us about a time you delivered a challenging piece of work."

- "Describe a situation where you had competing priorities."

- "How do you manage tight deadlines?"

- "Give an example of achieving a difficult outcome."

What panels are listening for:

- Planning skills

- Persistence

- Adaptability

- Accountability

Preparation tip: Have examples with clear outcomes, not just activity.

Productive Working Relationships

These questions explore how you work with others. They are about collaboration, influence, and professionalism.

Examples include:

- "Tell us about a time you worked with a difficult stakeholder."
- "Describe how you build relationships."
- "Give an example of working across teams."
- How do you handle conflict at work?"

What panels are listening for:

- Emotional intelligence
- Respect for others
- Ability to negotiate
- Willingness to listen
- Constructive problem solving

Preparation tip: Avoid blaming others. Show maturity and shared responsibility.

Drive, Integrity and Professionalism

These questions test your values and judgement. They are about how you behave when things are hard.

Examples include:

- "Describe a difficult ethical decision you've made."
- "How do you manage competing pressures?"
- "Give an example of where you demonstrated resilience."

What panels are listening for:

- Honesty
- Accountability
- Courage
- Reliability
- Alignment with APS Values

Preparation tip: Choose examples that show thoughtful judgement, not heroics.

Communicates with Influence

These questions examine how well you explain ideas, persuade others, and adapt your communication.

Examples include:

- "Tell us about a time you had to influence others."
- "Describe how you tailor communication to different audiences."
- "Give an example of delivering difficult messages."
- "How have you gained buy in for an idea?"

What panels are listening for:

- Clear structure
- Audience awareness
- Confidence without arrogance
- Ability to explain complexity simply

Preparation tip: Include examples with senior stakeholders where appropriate.

Technical and Role Specific Capability

These assess whether you can actually do the work.

Examples include:

- "Describe your experience with [specific system/process/policy]."
- "How would you approach completing [technical task]?"
- "What is your understanding of [relevant legislation/framework]?"
- "Talk us through how you would manage [core responsibility]."

What panels are listening for:

- Practical knowledge
- Application of skills
- Understanding of standards
- Ability to learn

Preparation tip: Link technical answers to real examples wherever possible.

Answering questions using STAR and STAR +

Use the STAR and STAR+ frameworks outlined in Chapter 5 to structure your answers, and then practise, practise, practise.

If we met in a café and you asked me how my weekend was and I responded with *"The situation was my wife was going out for dinner so the task I needed to complete was to make sure our boys were fed, entertained and put to bed. The actions I took were…"*

You would be looking at me the way you're looking at the page now. It's awkward in everyday conversation, but the STAR framework is incredibly helpful for peak performance in an interview.

Remember, we can't control the process so we're not going to worry about it. Playing by the rules dramatically increases your chances of success.

As a reminder, STAR stands for Situation, Task, Action, Result. STAR+ stands for Strategic Impact, Thinking, Applicability and Reflection.

You don't have to use these exact words to start each sentence and there is more information on using these frameworks starting on page 108.

Used well they enhance your answers by giving them more depth and further demonstrating your capabilities.

Exercise: Practice Out Loud

It can be useful to practise your answers out loud rather than writing them out and reading them in your head. They will sound different when you hear them spoken through. One way to do this is to ask someone, or a group of people, you trust to listen to your answer/s and then ask you questions about your answer.

It is important that you don't answer these questions at the time but that you write the questions down and the next time you give the answer you address the things they were curious or unsure about.

Thanks to my colleague Kylie F. for this great activity.

Handling Scenario Based Questions Without Guesswork

Scenario questions are becoming more prevalent in APS interviews. They often sound like:

- What would you do if a stakeholder pushed back?

- How would you manage multiple competing priorities?

- How would you approach a complex briefing request?

These questions can feel uncomfortable because they invite speculation. You could say almost anything, and without real context it is easy to drift into hypotheticals that don't show your capability. Panels don't want made up stories as answers to these questions. They want to understand your judgement and see evidence that you have handled similar situations before.

A simple and reliable way to answer these questions is to use a two step approach.

Step one: Give a clear, concise statement of what you would do.

Just the headline, one or two sentences that show your thinking and reassure the panel that you understand the intent of the question.

For example:

In that situation I would clarify the urgency, check the dependencies and communicate early with the stakeholder so expectations are aligned.

Step two: Pivot into a real STAR example.

This is where your answer becomes grounded, credible and assessable. You might say something like, *That's the same approach I took when…* and then walk them through a STAR example that demonstrates the exact behaviour they're asking about.

This pivot does two very important things. First, it avoids the trap of hypotheticals that are harder for everyone. Second, it brings the interview back into familiar STAR territory where you can shine through real evidence.

Here's what a combined answer might sound like:

If a stakeholder pushed back on a deadline, I would acknowledge their concern, clarify the constraints and work with them to agree on an approach that still meets our obligations. That's the same approach I took when I was coordinating the quarterly briefing pack for my Division. One of our key contributors advised they couldn't meet the deadline and I need it to be met. So I ...

And then you continue with your STAR example.

This structure works for almost any scenario question because it gives the panel both your judgement and your proven experience. The scenario provides the frame, the STAR example provides the evidence.

With practice, this becomes one of the easiest types of questions to answer. You don't need to invent a perfect response, one solid sentence about your approach, followed by a real example that shows how you already operate in a similar situation will get the job done. Panels appreciate this because it keeps the conversation grounded, honest and anchored in behaviour, not imagination.

If you don't have a STAR example that you can share then you can talk about what you would do in the situation and keep it as close as possible to what you would actually do. Then after the interview talk to your manager or look for opportunities to take on a task that will give you a real STAR example to address that question.

No matter the question having a good structure you can adapt your examples when providing your answer is key. If you fully script your answers you create challenges and difficulties for yourself that you don't need, let's look at what some of these are.

Why Fully Scripted Answers Usually Work Against You

Writing out full, word for word answers and trying to memorise them makes your life harder. While on the surface, this feels sensible because if I know exactly what I'm going to say, I'll feel more confident. If I practise it enough, I won't forget it. If I have the perfect answer ready, I'll perform better. Unfortunately, the opposite it more likely to happen for the following reasons.

Scripted Answers Sound Scripted

Panels hear lots of answers to interview questions and they become very good at recognising when someone is reciting something they have memorised. As they usually sound:

- Over polished
- Unnaturally structured
- Slightly stiff
- Lacking warmth
- Detached from the moment

Even when the content is strong, it feels rehearsed rather than genuine. Panels are not looking for performances, they want to get to know you and who you are.

Reading in Your Head While You're Talking

When you rely on scripted answers, what happens is instead of listening fully to the question and responding, part of your brain is trying to remember the "right" answer.

You are mentally reading while speaking, which uses up cognitive energy. It makes you slower, more anxious, and more likely to lose your place. Which means you are likely to:

- Rush,
- Repeat phrases,
- Lose eye contact, or
- Get flustered mid sentence.

Not because you lack capability, but because you are juggling too much in your head.

The "Close But Not Quite" Trap

One of the biggest risks of scripting is what happens when the question is similar to your prepared answer, but not the same.

For example:

You prepare a perfect answer for:

"Tell us about a time you worked with a difficult stakeholder."

In the interview you are asked:

"Tell us about a time you worked with a difficult team member."

They are related but they are not the same question. If you are working from a script, you will often try to force your stakeholder answer into the team member question. To do this you need to adjust on the fly which means you might:

- Skip parts,
- Add awkward explanations,
- Get parts wrong, or
- Apologise mid answer

The result is usually confusion, both for you and the panel.

Why This Is So Rattling

When this happens, people often feel thrown and left thinking *"I know this answer. Why can't I say it properly?"*

The problem is not their preparation, it's their rigidity. They prepared one narrow path instead of learning how to navigate the process using framework. To overcome this I recommend preparing talking points for your stories.

Prepare Stories, Not Scripts

A far more effective approach is to prepare flexible examples by knowing how to explain:

- The situation
- Your role
- The key actions
- The outcomes
- The learning

This allows you to adapt your example to different questions.

Assessment tasks

Sometimes during the recruitment process you'll be asked to complete an assessable task that is relevant to the role. Write a brief from some information, look at some IT code and debug it, analyse some financial reports and provide information. Approach these to the best of your ability and make sure you are clear on the instructions of the activity before you start and plan your approach to finish within the allocated time frame.

Random Questions and What Panels Are Really Looking For

Every now and then, an interview question seems to come out of left field. It doesn't sound like the usual capability based questions and it can catch you off guard.

Know that these questions aren't random for the sake of it. They're usually designed to reveal how you think, how you respond under pressure and how you make sense of your own behaviour.

Two questions I've heard asked are:

Tell us about a time you made a mistake and what you learned from it.

and

What's your favourite piece of technology and why?

Let's have a deeper look at both.

"Tell us about a time you made a mistake and what you learned from it"

This is one of my favourite interview questions, because it tells me a huge amount about the applicants self awareness, accountability and learning mindset.

The good news is that the actual mistake doesn't matter nearly as much as what you did next. You don't need a dramatic failure. In fact, please do not choose anything gross, illegal or wildly inappropriate. Sadly, I have seen candidates talk about hacking computer systems or getting caught stalking someone as part of a game at university and that is not the type of mistake that this question is looking for.

Also, and this is important, do not say you've never made a mistake. If you say that, you've just made a very big one in the interview. Panels are not testing whether you are perfect. They are testing whether you are honest and reflective, if you say you haven't made a mistake you will not score highly for this question.

Structure

First, outline the mistake briefly by keeping your answer factual and proportionate. Don't over explain and don't dramatise it, then focus on the parts that matter most:

- how you realised a mistake had occurred
- what you did to fix it
- how you told your team and manager
- what you have changed to reduce the chance of it happening again

This shows courage, responsibility and professionalism. It also demonstrates that you learn from experience rather than getting defensive or hiding problems.

What panels are really listening for here is:

- Can you acknowledge when something goes wrong?
- Do you take ownership?
- Do you act to correct issues?
- Do you improve your practice over time?

Those qualities matter far more than the mistake itself.

"What's your favourite piece of technology and why"

This question can feel completely unrelated to the job and that's exactly why it can be unsettling. When I was asked it during an interview, I had no prepared answer and felt genuinely stuck.

I paused, took a breath and then talked about a pair of headphones I'd recently bought that personalised the sound based on how my ears responded to music. I explained why I liked them, what problem they solved for me and why that mattered. I must have done well enough because I got the job.

Once I was settled in, I asked why they asked that question. Spoiler! They weren't interested in the technology itself, they were checking whether I could quickly choose something, organise my thinking and explain why I'd made that choice.

In other words, they were assessing:

- decision making
- clarity of thinking
- ability to build a simple case
- communication under light pressure

Any piece of technology would have been fine. What mattered was whether I could make a decision and justify it in a coherent way.

What to Remember About These Questions

When a question feels odd or unexpected, try not to panic or overthink it. Panels are rarely looking for a "right" answer. They are usually exploring how you think, reflect and respond in the moment.

And just like with scenario questions, once you understand what's really being assessed, these questions stop feeling random and start feeling manageable.

It's okay to pause. It's okay to take a breath. It's okay to say, *"That's an interesting question, let me think for a moment."* Those few seconds can help you move from reacting to responding. It can be useful to understand why we feels stuck so we'll explore that next and then there's a few more tips on getting unstuck in the next section.

Getting unstuck

Even with the best preparation and planning it's common to get stuck, draw a blank or be unsure what to do in parts of the interview. The key is learning to identify this, practice a response you can fall back on and then being able to take those steps in the moment.

Using Emotional Intelligence

Emotional Intelligence, popularised by Daniel Goleman, is at its core about recognising and managing our own emotional state, especially under pressure. Interviews are a perfect example of needing to do this. When the stakes feel high, your brain can interpret the situation as a threat, triggering what Goleman describes as an "amygdala hijack." The amygdala, the part of the brain responsible for detecting danger, jumps in and effectively overrides the prefrontal cortex, which is where your reasoning, language, and decision making sit making you feel stuck.

Physiologically, your body shifts into a survival response and stress hormones like adrenaline and cortisol are released, your heart rate increases, and blood flow is redirected away from the thinking parts of your brain toward the systems needed to react quickly. This is why, in an interview, you might suddenly go blank, lose your train of thought, or struggle to find words you know you have. It often shows up as flight or freeze. You might rush your answers to escape the moment, or freeze entirely and feel stuck mid sentence. Less commonly, it can show up as fight, becoming defensive, or fawn, over pleasing the panel through complements or positive comments. Understanding what's happening in your body can be reassuring. It's not that you don't know the answer, it's that your brain has temporarily prioritised survival over articulation.

"Between stimulus and response there is
a space.
In that space is our power to choose our
response.
In our response lies our growth and our
freedom"
- Viktor Frankl
Man's Search for Meaning

In an interview, that might be a challenging question or the surge of nerves that follows it. Practice noticing that moment rather than being swept up in it and take actions that help you reclaim just enough of that space for your thinking brain to come back online. It won't remove the nerves entirely, but it can shift you from reacting on autopilot to responding with intention.

Some things that can help you when you realise you are stuck are:

- Pause and breathe
- Ask to hear the question again
- Take a sip of water
- Go back to the structure you have practiced

Let's look at each in detail.

Pause and breathe

Often, we forget to breathe in interviews as we are nervous. Remember the panel want you to do well, the panel are trying to take notes and the panel know you are human. So, breathe and give everyone, including yourself a few seconds to catch up.

Ask to hear the question again

Ask for the question to be repeated and write some notes down, what information are the panel seeking from that question, what's an example you can share with them?

Take a sip of water

Having a drink nearby can help you to find a few seconds to pause and collect your thoughts.

Go back to the structure you have practiced

Think about the structure you are using to answer the question and move to the next step of it. For example, if you are stuck in describing why the level is attractive move to the role, if you are stuck describing the task, take a breath and say "the actions that I took were…" Both you and the panel will be right back on track.

Getting Unstuck Toolkit

Tick the ones that help you get unstuck, there's space to add your own if you would like:

[ ] Pause and breathe

[ ] Ask to hear the question again

[ ] Take a sip of water

[ ] Go back to structure you have practiced

[ ]

[ ]

[ ]

[ ]

[ ]

[ ]

[ ]

[ ]

Things to avoid doing during the interview

No matter how well prepared you are, there are certain behaviours and responses that hiring managers view as "red flags." These are not about one or two slip-ups; they reflect patterns that cause interviewers to doubt your fit, professionalism, or ability to work effectively with others.

Eva Chan in HBR suggests there are four main areas that cause concern and that you should actively avoid. They are:

- Being less than truthful
- Rude language or behaviour
- Criticising past employers or colleagues
- Not being prepared

Adapted from https://hbr.org/2024/10/the-4-interview-red-flags-hiring-managers-say-concern-them-most

Being Less Than Truthful

Dishonesty is the biggest red flag, by a significant margin. This doesn't only mean outright lying, it can also look like:

- Inflating your role on a project or overstating results.
- Listing skills you can't convincingly discuss with examples.
- Having inconsistencies between your resume, LinkedIn, and your interview answers.

Panels often check for consistency across sources, and even small discrepancies can make them question your credibility. If you can't back up something you've claimed with a specific example or detail, that's a signal you may have gone too far. Be honest, be accurate, and make sure everything you present is defensible.

Remember, even if you manage to sound like you were involved in your interview, the panel are likely to check this with your referee as well and you may get found out.

Rude Language or Behaviour

How you speak and act matters as much as what you say. Over half of hiring managers see poor language or discourteous behaviour as a red flag.

Examples that raise concerns include:

- Being abrupt or dismissive in your responses.
- Displaying defensive or aggressive body language.
- Arriving late without communication or apology.

These cues don't just suggest poor manners. They also signal poor emotional intelligence and an inability to build rapport, two things panels are constantly evaluating. Even small gestures and tone of voice contribute to an impression of how you might behave on the job.

The panel are often looking for a mix of both aptitude and attitude. It's not enough to be able to do the job well if you demonstrate behaviours that indicate you'll be difficult to work with, the panel will include that in their assessment.

Criticising Past Employers or Colleagues

Negative talk about past work environments might feel human, but it almost always backfires. Many hiring managers view complaining about previous employers or teams as a sign of poor professionalism or a fixed mindset.

Even when you've genuinely experienced friction or disappointment, focus on what you learned or how you adapted. For example, instead of saying, *"My previous team didn't support me,"* you could say, *"That experience taught me the importance of clear communication and helped me build better skills to collaborate."* Panels want to see resilience, adaptability, and maturity, not blame, excuses or denial.

Not being prepared

I trust at this point in the book I don't have to labour this point too much. Being unprepared and not knowing about the organisation, the role or what you would bring to it is not acceptable.

This is different to being nervous or not answering as smoothly as you would like. Hopefully, by being better prepared you are able to better manage these but they may still show up and that's ok.

Aptitude and Attitude

It's worth remembering that the interview doesn't start when you sit down in front of the panel, it starts the moment you walk into the building. From the security guard at the front desk to the person who greets you or escorts you to the room, every interaction is part of the impression you create. Being professional and courteous with everyone you meet shows consistency in how you carry yourself, not just when it matters most. These small interactions are noticed and sometimes even fed back to the panel. Treat each moment as part of the interview, and you'll show up in a way that feels natural, respectful, and aligned with the role you're aiming for.

Remember, panels are not just assessing your technical ability. They are trying to see who will *fit well into the team and organisation*. They are reading between the lines, watching for emotional intelligence, professionalism, and integrity. Avoiding these red flags doesn't guarantee a job offer, no one thing does, but it does ensure that you aren't undermining your chances by accident.

I've been on panels where applicants presented well in the interview and their answers scored highly. After they left though the only question the panel had was *"would I like to sit next to them for 40 hours a week?"*

Sometimes the answer was *"no, I wouldn't."* Their aptitude was great, but their attitude was poor and that influenced the decision made by the panel so make sure you display professional behaviour during the process.

Questions to Ask the Panel

Asking questions at the end of your interview isn't just a polite formality, it's part of the assessment of fit. It shows that you're thinking about what it would actually be like to do the job and to work with these people. Good questions are curious and forward looking rather than transactional. Even if you're nervous, asking one thoughtful question signals engagement, maturity and confidence, and it leaves the interview on a note of professional curiosity rather than simple relief that it's over.

Three questions to ask

Ask questions that give you further information, demonstrate your excitement about the role and that you're the right person for the job. The three questions I like to ask are:

If I am successful is winning the role, what would I be expected to have achieved in the first 6 months?

Or

What do you like about working here?

Or

What do you like to do after work?

If I was successful is winning the role, what would I be expected to have achieved in the first 6 months?

The IF is incredibly important in this question, if you start the question with WHEN it sounds arrogant and presumptive.

You might also outline what you think some priorities are to show you've thought about the role and then ask for more information. Especially, at more senior levels where you need to demonstrate higher levels of strategic thinking.

The answer to this question gives you two pieces of valuable information:

1. Is it the role that you think you applied for. It reads great on paper but when your potential future manager explains it to you in the interview it might sound different.
2. If you have forgotten something that is relevant the panel are likely to mention it. If they mention stakeholder engagement, project management, or outcome delivery then you can quickly explain your relevant skills and experience which can be included in the process.

What do you like about working here?

This question gives you a read on organisational culture and team dynamics. The answer "the coffee in the nearby cafe is good" or "the carparking is free" or "I live nearby" can be signs that you might need to explore further. The answers I want to this question include elements of "we get things done", "we make an impact", "we have fun" or "I get to learn a lot". You'll have your own markers for success to look out for.

The other thing this question does is gives the panel an opportunity to talk about themselves. From the panel members perspective they have:

- Read 100+ applications for the position (Assuming 5 minutes per application that's nearly 8 1/2 hours)

- Found 5-10 good ones and negotiated agreement on who to interview with the other panel members

- Sat in potentially 5-10 hours of interviews (another two whole work days) in between which they score about the interviews or run for water, food, tea, coffee, or a toilet break.

This question gives panel members a chance to talk about themselves and their experience. What they enjoy and why they are passionate about the work they do and the organisation they work for.

People often hold the assumption that you won't get a real answer to this question. I've had a panel member tell me the answers above. I've also had someone say "I'm two years from retirement, I get paid more here than I would anywhere else, I'm here for my super." So I'm happy to keep asking it as I can't control the answers they give me but I can control that I've asked the question.

What do you like to do after work?

Adapted from: https://hbr.org/2023/04/ask-this-question-at-the-end-of-your-next-job-interview

At first glance, this might sound casual or even irrelevant. In reality, it can tell you a great deal about the culture you are stepping into. This question gently shifts the conversation away from formal role requirements and towards how people actually experience their working lives.

Pay close attention not just to the words, but to the energy behind the response and this question can give you insight into:

Working hours

If answers consistently reference late nights, catching up on emails, or "finally logging off," it may signal long or unpredictable hours.

Burnout levels

Hesitation, jokes about exhaustion, or vague answers can point to fatigue and overload.

Team culture

Do people talk about family, sport, hobbies, volunteering, or rest? This often reflects whether wellbeing is genuinely valued.

Boundaries

You may learn whether people feel able to switch off or whether work regularly follows them home.

It also humanises the conversation. You are no longer just a candidate being assessed. You are professionals exploring whether this environment fits your life, values, and priorities.

Remember, recruitment is a two-way process. This question helps you assess not just whether you can do the job, but whether you can do it sustainably.

I don't like these questions

Some people don't like these questions and that's fine, ask the ones that work for you. I have had great success with them and will continue asking them. If you're going to ask a different question please don't ask the ones from the next section as they are not good questions and are frustrating to hear and answer as a panel member.

What **NOT** to ask

There are a number of questions that are frequently asked by people being interviewed because they have been told they need to ask a question. I will give you the answers to some commonly asked and not that useful questions that panels get asked.

Q: How many people applied?

A: We can't tell you.

Actual Answer: Why does it matter and how does it influence what's just happened? There's nothing you can do differently if they told you 2 people or 200 people applied so why would you care.

Q: When do you hope to let people know the outcome?

A: As soon as possible.

Actual Answer: We're under the pump already and a person down which is why we're hiring.

Note: If you are going to be away or difficult to contact in the weeks following the interview and you're asking this question to check whether things are likely to align. Just tell them and explain how they can best reach out to you if required.

Q: Is there anything from my earlier answers you'd like me to expand on?

A: No, I've got what I need.

Actual Answer: There is but I can't tell you because if I do I have to help everyone else in the process to keep it fair and I don't want to do that.

See the first question to ask in the section above to potentially get access to this information.

Q: How much will I get paid? How much leave will I get?

A: This amount of $. This amount of leave.

Actual Answer: You should just look that up on the website or often it's already in the job description. I thought you had good attention to detail and were self reliant and resourceful. Was I wrong?

Please don't ask these questions. In fact, you don't need to because I've told you what the answers are.

Where do I take this glass of water?

One final, very practical tip for face to face interviews. If there's a glass of water on the table, ask what you should do with it when the interview finishes. It sounds small, but it matters.

When you ask, you'll usually get one of two responses. Either, Leave it, we'll take care of it, or When Bailey comes to get you, they'll take you past the kitchen and you can pop it in the dishwasher. Either way, the act of asking shows consideration and awareness of the people around you.

I've sat through plenty of interviews where candidates talked about being thoughtful, collaborative and respectful of others, and then walked out leaving their mess for someone else to clean up. It's a small behaviour, but behaviours are exactly what panels are there to assess.

To be clear, if the rest of the interview hasn't gone well, this won't get you across the line. But if it has gone reasonably well and you're close to another strong candidate, small signals of professionalism and courtesy can genuinely make a difference.

And one more practical note. If you bring a water bottle, coffee cup or any rubbish into the room, take it with you when you leave.

Again, this doesn't work for everyone. It's unlikely that you'll be asked to take the glass anywhere and the panel usually sort it out. That being said I'm asking because I'm prepared to do whatever they ask me to do with it.

Chapter Summary

Interviewing well is about thinking clearly, communicating honestly, and demonstrating how you approach your work when it matters. When you understand the structure of interviews, prepare flexible examples, and trust your frameworks, you give yourself the best possible chance to be assessed fairly and accurately.

Throughout this chapter, we have explored how to answer common questions, respond to scenarios, manage unexpected moments, and leave a strong professional impression. You have also seen why presence, adaptability, and authenticity consistently matter more than polished scripts.

Even with strong preparation and solid performance, outcomes are never fully within your control. Sometimes you will be successful. Sometimes you will not. In both cases, every interview contains valuable information about your strengths, your gaps, and your readiness for future opportunities.

Chapter 9 outlines a process on to reflect after an interview in a structured and constructive way. You will learn how to review your performance without self criticism, identify practical learning points, and turn each experience into momentum rather than disappointment. This final step completes the cycle, helping you grow more confident and capable with every application you submit.

CHAPTER 9:
After the interview

Once an interview is over, most people move quickly into judgement mode. They replay moments in their head, fixate on answers they wish they had phrased differently, and scan for signs that they "messed up". This can happen before they have even walked back to their car.

While this reaction is understandable, it is rarely helpful. Interviews are complex, high pressure conversations. You are thinking, listening, responding, managing nerves, and trying to demonstrate capability all at once. No one does this perfectly, and in good news, perfection is not what panels are looking for.

Deliberate reflection allows you to step out of automatic self criticism and into learning. It gives you space to notice what worked, what felt strong, and where you can improve. Over time, this turns interviews from stressful one off events into stepping stones for growth.

There is also a well documented psychological tendency called negativity bias. Our brains naturally pay more attention to what went wrong rather than what went well. This can show up as replaying one awkward sentence while ignoring forty minutes of solid, competent answers.

"Reflection turns disappointment into direction."

Left unchecked, negativity bias can quietly undermine your confidence. You start to believe you are "bad at interviews" when the evidence does not support that story. Structured reflection helps you counter this pattern by grounding your thinking in facts rather than feelings.

This journal is designed to help you reflect with honesty, balance, and kindness. It invites you to recognise your strengths, learn from challenges, and make small, practical adjustments for next time.

Post Interview Journal

Aim to write this within 24 to 48 hours of your interview, once your emotions have settled but the experience is still fresh. Choose a quiet moment and treat this as professional development rather than self assessment or critique.

Be specific. "I was terrible" is not helpful reflection. "I rushed my first example and didn't clearly explain the outcome" is more beneficial.

Pay particular attention to what went well. These are clues to what you should repeat and refine in future interviews because confidence grows through evidence of experience, not from hope.

When noting challenges, focus on behaviours and skills rather than personal traits. You are not "bad under pressure" however, you may need more practice pausing before answering. Aim to come up with something practical you can work on.

If you receive panel feedback, include it here. Even brief comments can be valuable when reviewed alongside your own reflections. Over time, patterns will emerge that help you target your preparation more effectively.

Reflection: Post Interview Journal

What went well:	
What challenged me:	
What will I do differently next time:	
Feedback from the panel: (if you get it)	

Download a copy of this worksheet at
apsrecruitmentgame.com.au

Chapter Summary

Thoughtful reflection turns every interview into a learning opportunity. By noticing what worked, understanding what challenged you, and identifying one or two areas to strengthen, you steadily build confidence and capability. Instead of starting from scratch each time, you carry forward insight, experience, and build trust in yourself.

This process also protects you from being your own harshest critic. When you balance honesty with perspective, you are far more likely to stay motivated, resilient, and engaged in your job search.

Interviews are rarely the final step in an APS recruitment process. For many roles, referee checks play a critical role in confirming capability, professionalism, and fit. In the next chapter, we shift our focus to how to actively engage your referees, prepare them well, and ensure this final stage works in your favour rather than being left to chance.

CHAPTER 10:
Referee Checks

Referee reports are usually (but not always) done after interviews for candidates that are close or likely to be put in the successful pool, and they can have a huge influence on the final decision. Panels use them to confirm consistency between your answers and actual performance, check culture fit and get a sense of how you show up day to day. A strong referee who knows your work and can speak clearly about your strengths can make a real difference.

*"A strong referee confirms your story.
A weak one quietly undermines it."*

The good news is that you have more influence over this stage than you might think. Preparing your referee well is not only allowed, it is expected. You don't have to script them, just set them up to represent you accurately and positively.

Choosing the Right Referee

Your referee should be someone who can talk about you in a way that aligns with the role you're applying for. That usually means a current or recent manager, but there are times when a project lead, team leader or senior colleague is the better choice. They need to be a person who will give an accurate but positive account of the way you work.

You want someone who:

- has seen your performance up close
- understands your strengths
- can give practical examples
- communicates clearly
- is reliable when contacted

Inside the Interview Room

I once called a referee for a candidate that had performed well in the recruitment process. They probably weren't going to be the preferred candidate but they were strong enough to be put in the merit pool. Our conversation started like this.

Me: Hi Geoff, my name is Brendon and I'm working for scribing company for an APS6 round at government department. Anthony has listed you as a referee and…

Geoff: Oh he's listed me has he, that's interesting.

Me: Are you prepared to give a report for me to include in the process?

Geoff: Yep, but it won't be a positive one.

The awkward conversation completed, I rang the panel chair and asked if they wanted me to check with the other referee, which they did. That call was thankfully a lot easier, and I hope someone told Anthony to not use Geoff as their referee anymore.

Reflection: Who will I ask to be my referee?

Who are the three people who could speak about you accurately and positively?

Referee 1	
Referee 2	
Referee 3	

Which of them knows your recent work best?

Let Them Know They Are Your Referee

It sounds obvious, but many people forget this step. Do not assume someone knows you have listed them as a referee, make sure you tell them. A quick conversation or email helps them prepare and makes the whole process smoother.

You might say:

I've applied for a role in [organisation], and I've listed you as my referee. The panel may contact you this week. I've attached the job ad, my selection criteria response and would appreciate if you could highlight (insert skills or area of focus here) when you are contacted.

This simple courtesy means your referee is not surprised, rushed or trying to remember details under pressure when they get a phone call and can do some preparation and hopefully you can see the value of that if you've read this far.

> **Tip:** You might want to wait until after your interview to reach out to them so that you can confirm what you'd like them to talk about and it is fresh in their mind when they are contacted.

What You Want Them To Focus On

Your referee is not expected to repeat your STAR examples word for word. Instead, they give the panel a sense of how you work consistently. This is your opportunity to gently guide their focus as required, you might highlight:

- the key strengths you want reinforced
- any capability the role emphasises, such as judgement, collaboration or prioritisation
- something you forgot to mention in the interview

For example, if you realised on the way home that you hardly spoke about stakeholder management, you can say:

One thing I didn't have time to sufficiently cover was my work with external stakeholders. If it comes up, feel free to mention the work we did with the data governance group.

You're not coaching them to exaggerate, you're helping them recall the most relevant parts of your work together.

What Panels Are Looking For

Again, panels aren't looking for perfection, they are looking for alignment and consistency. Most referee checks explore:

- how you collaborate
- your reliability
- your performance at level
- your integrity
- how you handle pressure or complexity
- your communication style
- whether you behave the way you described in your interview

If your referee reinforces the patterns you showed in your interview and selection criteria, that creates a strong sense of confidence for the panel.

If You Are Worried About a Referee

Everyone has had a tricky professional relationship at some point. If you are concerned about how a previous manager might represent you, you can:

- choose a different referee who has supervised your work

- explain the context to the panel if they specifically request your current manager
- offer an additional referee who has seen your performance more recently
- offer for them to speak to your manager's manager.

Panels understand that workplaces are complex. Choosing someone who can speak clearly and fairly is always better than choosing someone who will feel uncomfortable being contacted.

Inside the Interview Room

I once applied for a role where the interview went well, and the panel asked to contact my current manager as a referee. My current manager and I did not have a strong working relationship and I was concerned their feedback would not be accurate of my actual ability or very positive.

The panel respected my transparency. They contacted an alternative referee, received an accurate and positive report, and I was offered the role.

Worksheet: Referee Preparation

Referee name:	
Strengths I'd like them to highlight:	
Two examples I'll remind them of:	
Anything I forgot to emphasise in the interview:	

Download a copy of this worksheet at
apsrecruitmentgame.com.au

Chapter Summary

Referee checks work best when they reinforce the story you have already told through your application and interview. When your referee understands the role, knows your strengths, and feels prepared to speak about your work, they become a powerful advocate for you. This is about clarity, respect, and professional courtesy.

By choosing wisely, communicating early, and guiding focus thoughtfully, you increase the likelihood that this final stage reflects you accurately and positively.

Even when you do everything well, however, outcomes are not guaranteed. Strong candidates are sometimes unsuccessful for reasons outside their control. In the next chapter, we turn to what to do when you don't get the job, how to respond constructively, and how to use disappointment as fuel for future success rather than a reason to doubt yourself.

CHAPTER 11:
When you don't get the job

Sometimes, despite doing everything "right", you won't get the job. Not being successful can sting, it can shake your confidence and trigger a flood of second guessing. You might find yourself replaying every answer, every pause, thinking about every moment you wish you could redo, go back to your post interview journal and look at what went well.

The Panel's decision is shaped by timing, internal priorities, team dynamics, budget, and most likely the presence of another candidate who happens to fit this particular role more closely at this particular moment.

This chapter is about helping you respond to disappointment with perspective. It is about learning without self blame, rebuilding confidence, and staying engaged with the process rather than withdrawing from it.

What should I have done?

In many cases, there genuinely isn't much more you could have done. You prepared well, you answered clearly, you showed your capability, and you still came second to someone who simply had stronger experience, more directly relevant skills or a closer match to what the panel needed right now. That's disappointing especially when you really wanted the job and worked hard to put your best foot forward.

Getting useful feedback can help, but it can also be frustratingly difficult. Panels often interview a lot of candidates in a short period of time, and the feedback you receive may feel vague. You might hear things like *you need to be more strategic* or *you didn't quite align with what we were looking for*. Sometimes that feedback is helpful, often it isn't.

When the feedback is broad or unclear, I encourage you to trust your own reflections more. Think about what you were proud of, what you would tweak next time, and then move on. Don't let the outcome define you.

I like to think about recruitment a bit like buying a house at auction. There are lots of strategies people talk about to win at auction. Open with a strong bid, fire back quickly in response to others, wait until the last moment and jump in. But in the end, only one strategy actually guarantees you'll win. Have the most money and be prepared to spend it on that particular house. That's it, that's how you win at auction.

In recruitment occasionally you simply bump into someone who has more currency for that particular role at that particular time. More experience in that domain, more exposure to that type of work, or a background that aligns more closely with what the panel is seeking. The good news is, their "money" is now out of the market. You don't have to compete with them for the next role as hopefully they're enjoying their new role and aren't applying for jobs anymore.

If you're consistently getting interviews, that's a strong signal you are competitive and you're in the game. Each application and interview builds your experience, your confidence and your readiness. The aim isn't to win every time. It's to stay in the game long enough, and be prepared enough, that when the right role comes along, you're ready to step forward and take it.

Chapter Summary

Not getting the job is rarely a judgement on your value or potential and most often reflects factors that sit well beyond your control.

When feedback is available, use it thoughtfully. Look for patterns rather than isolated comments. When feedback is vague or unhelpful, trust your own reflections. Focus on what you handled well, what you learned, and what you would approach differently next time.

If you are regularly being shortlisted and interviewed, you are doing many things right. You are visible, are presenting as credible and you are competitive. Each application and interview builds experience, clarity, and confidence.

Recruitment is not about winning every time. It is about staying in the game long enough, and developing enough, that when the right opportunity appears, you are ready to step forward with conviction.

In the next chapter, we will step back and look at the recruitment process as a whole. We will walk through the key stages, explain what typically happens at each point, and answer some common questions. Understanding the mechanics of the process can reduce uncertainty and help you approach future opportunities with greater calm and confidence.

CHAPTER 12:
Key steps and FAQs

You have identified your next move, found a good role and three fits match, determined your achievements, prepared a strong application, practiced to perform well in interviews, engaged your referees, and responded constructively when things do not go to plan.

You may still be uncertain about particular parts of the process. Recruitment can feel opaque from the outside and different organisations do things slightly differently. It is easy to feel unsure about what is happening, what is normal, and what you should reasonably expect at each stage.

This chapter brings the whole process together. It outlines the key stages of APS recruitment and answers the questions people regularly ask. Hopefully this helps you understand how the system works so you can approach future opportunities with greater clarity and confidence.

Key APS Recruitment Steps

Job Advertisement

The job advertisement is your first window into the role, the team, and what the panel is really looking for. It outlines the key responsibilities, capability expectations, essential and desirable criteria, and practical details such as location and tenure. Reading it carefully helps you decide whether the role fits you and how to tailor your application.

Positions are advertised on **APSjobs.gov.au** and sometimes via agency websites, LinkedIn, Seek.com or internal job boards (you can only access these if you work internally already).

Application

The application is where you present your evidence on paper. This usually includes your resume, a pitch or statement, and sometimes responses to selection criteria. Its purpose is to show, clearly and convincingly, that you meet the requirements and deserve to progress to the next stage.

Shortlisting

Shortlisting is where the panel reviews applications and decides who will be interviewed. They compare the evidence provided against the role requirements and rank candidates based on merit.

Assessment

Assessment includes all methods used to evaluate your suitability for the role. This may involve written tasks, presentations, psychometric testing, work samples, or referee reports. Each activity is designed to gather evidence of your capability at the required level. This is more common in roles where technical skills are required (finance, legal, communications, IT, etc.)

Interview

The interview is your opportunity to bring your application to life. Panels use questions to test your experience, judgement, and behaviours against the ILS and role requirements. This is where preparation, clear examples, and calm delivery matter most.

Reference Checks & Security Clearance

At this stage, panels verify your claims and assess your reputation through referees and security checks. Referees are asked about your performance, reliability, and conduct, while clearances confirm your suitability to work in sensitive environments.

Offer & Onboarding

If you are the preferred candidate and all checks are satisfactory, you will receive a formal offer. Onboarding then supports your transition into the role through inductions, training, and introductions to systems and people. A strong start here sets the foundation for your success in the role.

Common APS Recruitment Questions

What does APS6 or EL1 mean?

APS roles are classified from APS 1–6, EL1, EL2, SES Band 1–3.

Each level has defined responsibilities, capability requirements, and pay ranges.

What is merit selection?

Merit means choosing the candidate/s whose skills, knowledge, and experience best match the job requirements.

What are bulk recruitment rounds?

Bulk rounds are used when agencies need to fill many similar roles at once and assess a large group of candidates through the same process. Successful applicants may be placed into multiple teams or locations from the same recruitment activity.

How competitive are APS jobs?

Popular roles, especially EL1–EL2 and SES positions, often attract dozens to hundreds of applicants.

What is a panel interview?

A selection panel typically includes 2–3 people who assess candidates against capabilities and values. They may ask scenario-based or behavioural questions. Usually the panel is comprised of the manager of the team, a senior member of the team and an independent person from another part of the organisation.

What is a recruitment panel's role?

The recruitment panel is responsible for assessing candidates against the advertised role requirements using evidence from applications, interviews and referee reports. Their job is to apply the assessment criteria consistently and make a recommendation to the delegate.

What is a panel chair's role?

The panel chair leads the recruitment process and ensures it is fair, consistent and defensible. They manage the panel, guide discussions, keep the process on track and are ultimately responsible for the quality of the panel's recommendation to the delegate.

What does a scribe do?

A scribe takes detailed notes during interviews to accurately capture what candidates say. They do not assess candidates or influence decisions, their role is to support fairness, accuracy and consistency in the process. They are often asked to provide guidance on good recruitment practices and process given they have more exposure to recruitment activities than other panel members.

What is a delegate?

A delegate is the person with the formal authority to make the final recruitment decision. They usually sit outside the panel and rely on the panel's assessment and recommendations, although they can ask questions or seek clarification before approving the outcome.

How long does the process take?

It can range from weeks to months, depending on the role and agency and the number of applicants.

What is the difference between a merit list and a merit pool?

A merit list ranks candidates in order of suitability for a specific vacancy, with offers made from the top down. A merit pool is a group of candidates assessed as suitable who can be offered similar roles in the future, often across different teams or even agencies, within a set time period.

What is the difference between ongoing and non-ongoing positions?

Ongoing roles are permanent; non-ongoing roles are temporary, fixed-term, or project-based. Non-ongoing positions can lead to ongoing opportunities but it's not guaranteed.

What is a Section 26 transfer?

A Section 26 transfer allows an ongoing APS employee to move to another agency at the same classification level without going through a full competitive recruitment process. It still requires the receiving agency to be satisfied the person is suitable for the role, usually through an interview and referee checks.

What are identified positions?

An Identified position requires the candidate to have an understanding of the issues affecting Aboriginal and Torres Strait Islander peoples, and proven culturally appropriate engagement and communication skills. Typically these roles will involve the development of policies or programs targeted at Aboriginal and Torres Strait Islander people, or direct interaction with Aboriginal and/or Torres Strait Islander communities. Vacancies for these jobs are open to everyone.

Source: https://www.apsc.gov.au/sites/default/files/2021-03/indigenous-recruitment-guide_0.pdf

What is security clearance and do I need it?

Some roles require clearance (baseline, NV1/NV2, or higher). This involves background checks by the Australian Government Security Vetting Agency (AGSVA) to ensure suitability to handle sensitive information.

This process can take a while but you are not able to apply for a clearance before you have a job that requires it. You may or may not be able to start your role prior to gaining the appropriate clearance.

Chapter Summary

APS recruitment can seem complex, but at its core it follows a clear and consistent structure. Advertise, receive applications, shortlist, assess, interview, check, decide, and onboard. Each stage exists to gather evidence and support fair, merit based decisions.

Understanding this process gives you an advantage. It helps you prepare more effectively, interpret outcomes more accurately, and avoid taking delays or setbacks personally. It also allows you to engage with panels, referees, and recruiters in a calm, professional way.

Throughout this book, the focus has been on helping you show up as your best professional self. Thoughtful, prepared, reflective, and resilient.

If you take anything from these chapters, let it be this. You are not powerless in this process. With preparation, perspective, and practice, you can navigate it with confidence and integrity, and build a career that reflects who you are and what you value.

CHAPTER 13:
Beyond the APS

The approach you have built throughout this book is grounded in APS recruitment, yet the underlying principles extend well beyond it. Once you understand how to identify what a role requires, translate your experience into clear evidence, and communicate it with intent, you are working with skills that apply across a wide range of recruitment environments.

This chapter expands your perspective so you can carry that approach into different contexts with confidence. You will see what remains consistent across recruitment processes, where variation is likely to occur, and how to adjust without losing the structure and clarity you have developed. The aim is to help you stay anchored in a strong, repeatable approach while adapting to different systems, language and expectations.

Applying the Game More Broadly

While this book is grounded in recruitment within the Australian Public Service, the patterns, behaviours, and expectations you've been working with are not unique to the APS. They show up across state and territory governments, local councils, and even in international public sector and large organisational recruitment.

The systems may look different, the language might change and the process can feel less structured or, at times, more opaque. The game is still being played.

What stays the same

Across most recruitment processes, a few things consistently matter and these are things we've explored throughout the book.

Clarity of role

Organisations are looking for someone who understands what the role requires that can step into it with minimal friction.

Evidence of capability

Whether it's framed as selection criteria, capabilities, or competencies, you are being assessed on your ability to demonstrate past behaviour that predicts future performance.

Fit and judgement

Panels and hiring managers are asking themselves, "Can this person do the job?" and "Will they do it well here?"

Communication

Your ability to clearly articulate your experience, decisions, and impact is often the difference between being shortlisted and being overlooked.

These are not APS specific capabilities, they are recruitment fundamentals which provide a consistent foundation across recruitment processes and give you something stable to work from.

What changes

Where people often get caught is assuming the process will look the same everywhere and unfortunately it won't. There are a few things that you may need to adapt.

Integrated Leadership System (ILS) vs other frameworks

Different organisations use different capability frameworks. The names change, but the underlying expectations are often very similar and cover common topics such as leadership, communication, judgement, delivery.

Panels vs hiring managers

Even with the move from structured panels to more conversational interviews with one or two decision-makers the need to provide clear, relevant examples does not go away.

Process transparency

APS recruitment is relatively structured, other environments may feel less predictable. This increases the importance of your preparation and your ability to adapt in the moment.

How to apply what you've learned

Rather than starting again, think about how to translate your approach:

- Take the examples you've developed and adapt the language, not the substance
- Focus on outcomes and impact, not just process
- Prepare for variation, not perfection
- Stay anchored in your strategy, not just the mechanics of one system

Chapter Summary

Once you are clear on what a role requires, able to present strong evidence of your capability, and confident in how you communicate your experience, you can step into different recruitment environments without needing to start again.

Your focus is to adapt on the surface while holding onto the structure underneath. When you do this well, you move through different contexts with confidence, apply your thinking with intent, and give yourself a strong chance of success wherever you are applying.

CHAPTER 14:
Final Thoughts

If you have read this book from start to finish, you have chosen to approach your career thoughtfully rather than reactively. You have decided to understand the recruitment process rather than be at the mercy of it. You have invested time in learning how to present your experience clearly, reflect honestly, and respond constructively to both success and disappointment.

Too many capable people drift through recruitment feeling uncertain, underprepared, and quietly self critical. They submit applications at the last minute, or walk into interviews hoping for the best and then they take rejection personally. Over time, this erodes confidence and narrows ambition.

This book has been about offering you a different path. A path grounded in preparation rather than panic, reflection rather than rumination, learning rather than self blame and agency rather than helplessness.

By reading these chapters, you have explored how to understand roles properly, write compelling applications, prepare strong examples, engage thoughtfully with panels and referees, and respond with perspective when outcomes are not what you hoped for. You have learned how the system works, what panels are looking for, and where you can meaningfully influence the process.

You do not need to be perfect to succeed in recruitment, you need to be:

- Prepared,
- Reflective,
- Honest, and
- Willing to keep learning.

If this book has helped you feel clearer, steadier, and more confident about your next step, I'm excited for you and grateful you've taken the time to read and apply the things you've learned.

All the best and good luck playing the game.

FRAMEWORKS INDEX

ACTIVITIES INDEX

ABOUT THE AUTHOR

Brendon Le Lievre has spent his career helping people navigate the world of work with more confidence, clarity and humanity. With a background spanning HR, leadership development and people capability, Brendon has worked closely with teams and leaders across the Australian Public Service for many years.

He has chaired recruitment panels, supported hiring managers through complex staffing processes and seen firsthand what strong applications and candidates look like. As an external scribe to APS agencies, he has participated in more than 300 interviews, capturing evidence, analysing capability and observing how panels make decisions. These experiences have given him a rare window into what actually works in APS recruitment and what gets in the way.

Alongside this, Brendon has coached hundreds of APS staff to recruitment success. From graduates and early career applicants through to APS6, EL1,

EL2 and SES candidates, he has helped people strengthen their examples, build presence, understand their value and walk into interviews feeling prepared rather than overwhelmed.

Brendon brings a calm, practical and human-centred approach to the recruitment process. He believes selection criteria don't need to feel impossible to respond to, interviews don't need to be intimidating, and panels genuinely want applicants to do well. His work is grounded in clarity, structure and simple behavioural frameworks that remove guesswork and help people put the best version of themselves forward.

This book brings together everything he has learned from sitting on both sides of the table. It is designed to give you the tools, language and confidence to show your strengths clearly and step into opportunities that align with your skills, values and aspirations.

WORKING WITH BRENDON

If you've found this book helpful, here's some ways we can work beyond these pages.

I focus on helping people navigate the human side of work with more clarity, confidence and calm.

Career and recruitment coaching

Support to clarify your next step, identify relevant examples, prepare strong applications, and walk into interviews feeling grounded rather than rushed or rehearsed.

Transition support into new roles and levels

For people stepping into leadership roles, new policy environments or broader scopes of responsibility, helping them adjust their mindset, build influence and lead effectively at their new level.

The APS Recruitment Game Workshops

If you're looking to go beyond reading and put these ideas into practice, I run tailored workshops for teams and groups based on the concepts in this book. These sessions (face to face and virtual) are designed to help participants actively learn how to play the game, not just understand it. We work through real examples, unpack recruitment processes, and apply the strategies directly to your organisation's context so people can see what strong performance looks like and start building it themselves.

The workshops are interactive and grounded in real recruitment scenarios. Participants will have the opportunity to test their thinking, refine their approach, and get clear on how to position themselves with confidence. Whether you're supporting staff to prepare for their next role or building capability across a team, the focus is on practical tools that can be used immediately.

Leadership development for teams and agencies

Designing and facilitating practical leadership and wellbeing sessions that reflect the realities of public sector work, including managing competing priorities, building psychological safety, leading through complexity and practical leader as coach programs.

If you'd like support applying the ideas in this book to your own situation, or you're curious about working together, you can find more information about my current programs and how to get in touch at:

WWW.HARECONSULTING.COM.AU

Across all of this work, my approach is calm, practical and to have fun. I believe most people already have far more capability than they give themselves credit for. Often the real work is helping them slow down, make sense of what's happening, and choose their next steps with intention rather than pressure.

THE APS RECRUITMENT GAME